Reading
Lips

Reading Lips

And Other Ways to
Overcome a Disability

*Winners of the First Helen Keller Foundation for Research and Education
International Memoir Competition*

Edited by
Diane Scharper
and
Philip Scharper, Jr., M.D.

Apprentice House
Baltimore, Maryland
www.ApprenticeHouse.com

Library of Congress Cataloging-in-Publication Data

Scharper, Diane, 1942-
Reading lips : and other ways to overcome a disability /
Diane Scharper.
p. cm.
ISBN 978-1-934074-19-0
1. People with disabilities—Biography. 2. Quality of life.
I. Title.

HV1552.3.S33 2007
362.4092'2—dc22
2007031930

Printed in the United States of America

First Edition

Published by Apprentice House
The Future of Publishing...Today!

Apprentice House
Communication Department
Loyola College in Maryland
4501 N. Charles Street
Baltimore, MD 21210

410.617.5265
410.617.5040 (fax)
www.ApprenticeHouse.com
info@ApprenticeHouse.com

DEDICATION

This book is dedicated with love to my family
in gratitude for their immense help and support.

"Here, at whatever hour you come, you will find light and hope and human kindness."

Albert Schweitzer

(Guiding principle for the Retina Specialists of Alabama)

CONTENTS

FOREWORD

Great-Great-Aunt Helen
Keller Johnson Thompson

I remember the day vividly, when my grandmother, Patty Tyson Johnson, the niece of Helen Keller, came to share the story of Helen Keller with my fourth grade class.

Certainly my classmates and I knew that Helen Keller was a very special part of our little town, Tuscumbia, Alabama. After all, there is Helen Keller's birthplace and childhood home called "Ivy Green," The Helen Keller Public Library, and Helen Keller Hospital, just to name a few. How proud I was to learn that fateful day that Helen Keller not only touched our town, she changed our nation and our world by showing others what strength and courage are all about.

I was amazed to learn that my Aunt Helen's victory over her dark and silent world turned her life and her ambitions to the service of those in need. With energy and stamina that were almost limitless, she dedicated her life to others. She gave of herself unceasingly as she spoke, wrote, traveled, and worked constantly to improve the conditions of deaf and blind people.

For more than half a century, Helen Keller employed the symbol of her own courage and faith to benefit millions of her fellow handicapped in America and throughout the world. She not only inspired programs for the education and rehabilitation of blind people around the globe, she also graduated from college *Cum Laude*, learned to speak seven languages, and gave speeches in more than thirty-five countries on five continents.

Over the past twenty-seven years, it has been important for me to realize that Helen Keller would have never succeeded as she did without her teacher and companion of fifty years, Anne Sullivan Macy. There is no doubt that Aunt Helen was quite remarkable, extremely intelligent, sensitive, and determined, and certainly she was the first person with a disability to make such a public success of her life.

However, she has not been the only one who faced adversity and succeeded, as is evident in the twenty nine essays in this anthology. Their efforts prove that obstacles and hardships do not have to lead to failure. As Helen Keller once said, "In order for the light to shine so brightly, the darkness must be present."

Keller Johnson Thompson is Vice President of Education for the Helen Keller Foundation, based in Birmingham, Alabama.

PREFACE

An Everlasting Mark
Robert Morris

In 1987, we began collaborative eye research with a Swedish scientist, Magnus Hook, who had immigrated to the United States to work at the University of Alabama at Birmingham. One day he told us that he had studied Helen Keller in high school in Sweden and was surprised that it wasn't widely known that Alabama was Helen Keller's home state. He challenged us to begin eye research under the name of our state's most famous citizen.

In 1988, interested research scientists and physicians joined members of Helen Keller's family to start the Helen Keller Eye Research Foundation. Our first Chairman of the Board was Charley Boswell, a man who lost both eyes to battlefield injury during World War II. Mr. Boswell subsequently won twenty-eight United States and International blind golf championships. You might say that he was to blind golf what Arnold Palmer and Jack Nicklaus combined were to golf in general. Charley Boswell was our first leader and our first memoirist, chronicling his story in an autobiography titled *Now I See*, and describing his chairmanship of the Helen Keller Eye Research Foundation as his chance "to leave an everlasting mark."

By 1997, we realized that we wanted to conduct speech and hearing research as well. And equally importantly, we knew that we wanted to meet the public by teaching Helen Keller's entire life and legacy, which we had come to know and love through her family and her writing. Thus was born our final name—The Helen Keller Foundation for Research and Education—saving sight, speech, and hearing. Today this foundation unites her legacy with solutions to blindness and deafness by advancing research and education.

Educational activities allowed us to meet the public by employing Keller Johnson, Helen Keller's great-niece, to teach character education in elementary schools nationwide, based on Helen's story. An exciting new part of our education program is this collection of memoirs that truly carry on Helen Keller's life meaning. She taught the world to reconsider the remaining abilities of the disabled, and in doing so, she forever increased their life potential. Now these memoir authors, by their words and actions, are teaching that same lesson in her name.

For this additional opportunity to further Helen Keller's legacy, we will always be grateful to Diane Scharper and her supportive family. We thank the authors, and we look forward to many more inspiring stories of people who have walked in step with Helen Keller, the "first lady of courage."

Robert Morris, M.D., is Presdient of the Helen Keller Foundation for Research and Education.

ACKNOWLEDGMENTS

I am grateful to Robert Morris, M.D., for his vision in being the first to see the potential of recognizing those who have overcome disabilities and how their stories can inspire all of us—just as Helen Keller did.

I am also indebted to members of his staff at the Retina Specialists of Alabama, especially Margaret Harrill for her tremendous help with this project.

Thank you also to members of the Helen Keller Foundation for Research and Education including Lana Fields, Don Fletcher, M.D., the Daniel Foundation, the family of Helen Keller, the Board of Directors for the Helen Keller Foundation, and Philip Scharper, M.D., former fellow of the Retina Specialists of Alabama.

I am also grateful to Towson University for its support of this project, specifically Dr. Robert Caret, President of Towson University; Dr. Edwin Duncan, Chairman of the English Department; Geoffrey Becker, Director of the PRWR program; graduate students in the program, especially Joyce Hammock. Thank you also to Nancy Kavanaugh, former student and friend, and my family.

Finally, I want to thank the writers who submitted their work as well as their physicians who helped and, in some cases, healed them. The fruits of their labor are evident on these pages. Your wisdom, insights, time, good nature, patience, and kindness have paid off.

INTRODUCTION

On a Mission
Diane Scharper

> *The surgeon was bending over me saying, "I don't understand much of this, but I just removed a small benign tumor with some attached necrotic tissue that was located centerline in your brain. It appears this new cyst had cut off the blood supply that had been nourishing the inoperable cancer. And post operative x-rays indicate you are cancer free!"*
>
> *From some distant place, I heard myself mumbling, "After six surgeries and all this preparation to die, you're telling me I'm going to live"?*
> —Bradford Walker, "The Space Left Behind After Loss"

The incident occurred in October of 1985. Twenty years later, Mr. Walker not only lives but tells about his experience in his memoir in a chapter with the fitting title, "The Miracle." Mr. Walker's memoir was one that The Helen Keller Foundation for Research and Education received in response to a call for papers.

Announced in November, 2004, the Helen Keller memoir competition called for memoirs about overcoming disabilities written in poetry or prose of 3,000 words or fewer. By the June 1, 2005 deadline, the foundation received 284 entries, more than they had thought possible. Now those entries have been culled to twenty-nine memoirs which ironically are uplifting even though they're grounded in pain. That all of these pieces of writing record people who "live" with their disabilities, as opposed to merely "suffering" from them, is in itself a kind of miracle. Moreover, the memoirs ascribed success to those disabilities, believing themselves enabled, not disabled by them. Helen Keller also believed herself to be enabled by her disabilities and spent much of her life publicizing that belief. Because she talked about her blindness and deafness, she changed the way people thought about all disabilities. Before her time, disabilities were hidden and not discussed. Moreover the example of her life empowered disabled people and inspired the rest of the world, to say nothing of Dr. Robert Morris, a retina surgeon and the president of the Helen Keller Foundation.

I met Dr. Morris several years ago when we discussed the memoir project, which would feature a call for memoirs about overcoming disabilities. As we talked, the conversation drifted to the topic of miracles and to a miracle that took place in May, 2002. Strictly defined, it wasn't a miracle so much as it was a healing that stemmed from scientific advances in the field of ophthalmology. As Dr. Morris talked about that healing, he pointed out the painting that hung on a wall outside his operating room. A gift from the sister of a blind man whose sight Dr. Morris had restored to 20/50 "newspaper reading vision," the painting depicted an actual miracle: the story of Jesus curing a blind man as seen in John 9: 1-41.

Dr. Morris put his hand over Jesus' hand saying that he sometimes makes this gesture before he operates as a way of praying for the operation's success. As he touched his hand to the painting, Dr. Morris refreshed my memory of the story in which Jesus, taking mud and saliva, pastes the mixture on the blind man's eyes telling him to wash his face, and his vision would be restored. Astonished by the miraculous healing, a crowd asks who was to blame for the man's blindness, his parents—by some misdeed—or himself. Dr. Morris paused as he recounted Jesus' answer: "Neither this man nor his parents sinned; he was born blind so that God's work might be revealed in him."

That statement, Dr. Morris explained, is one that would serve as the inspiration for a memoir anthology and one that Helen Keller would second wholeheartedly. Immortalized in William Gibson's 1989 play, "The Miracle Worker," a moment occurs when Helen Keller realizes that all things have a name. Blind and deaf since eighteen months of age when a bout with meningitis shut her off from the world, seven-year-old Helen Keller (1880-1968) stands beside the pump outside her home in Tuscumbia, Alabama, and feels water rush into her open hand.

"Suddenly I felt a misty consciousness as of something forgotten—a thrill of returning thought—and somehow the mystery of language was revealed to me. I knew then that 'w-a-t-e-r' meant the wonderful cool something that was flowing over my hand. That living word awakened my soul, gave it light, hope, joy, set it free!"

Ultimately, with the help of her teacher, Annie Sullivan, Helen Keller became the first blind-deaf person to effectively communicate with the outside world. An international celebrity from the age of eight, Helen Keller announced in 1909 after graduating from college that her life would be dedicated to the amelioration of blindness. She visited thirty-five countries on five continents; wrote fifteen books; contributed articles to various periodicals; and received many civic, national, and international awards including a Presidential Medal of Freedom and several honorary doctorates.

With a goal to save sight, speech, and hearing, The Helen Keller Foundation was formed in 1988 by members of Helen Keller's family and a group of distinguished scientists and physicians. It took as its purpose Helen Keller's challenge: "Help me to hasten the day when there shall be no more blindness."

Hoping to publicize their national and international efforts to further the knowledge necessary to treat diseases of the eye, the Helen Keller Foundation announced a memoir competition. The entries came from all over the world, not just the United States where it had been advertised. From Scotland, Australia, New Zealand, India, Indonesia, Africa, and Israel, writers described a wide range of disabilities from overcoming the effects of blindness to dealing with cancer and its effects. Most of the entrants wrote about their own experiences, although several wrote about the experiences of their children or their siblings. One even described her sister's successful efforts to walk despite her bout with crippling polio:

> In addition to letters, gifts and cards, I sent my sister the same urgent mental affirmation, thought and prayer over and over and over again: "Walk, Jeanette, WALK."
> —Judith Stevens Allison, "The Bravest Sister of All"

But all the stories had one thing in common. Whether by force of will, prayer, or love, each writer had found an inner resource that had not just helped him cope. He had transformed his life and given it a whole new meaning, suggesting that people could survive their pain not merely endure it, and by surviving, they could show the supposedly able-bodied the solid bedrock of that most spiritual essence, the soul.

On a mission: that's how most of the writers put it. They had a mission in life, one they realized only after they confronted their disabilities. This is perhaps why an anthology so filled with human suffering—much of it still going on—is also filled with hope and ineffable *joi de vivre*.

PART ONE

Reading Lips

Disability Ongoing

Reading Lips
Amy Alznauer

Forgive my fingers pressed against your face
To hear by catching the force of air
Expressed, each little stretch, each grimace
And slack, as if by touch I mean to stare.

So intimate for one drawn back by sight,
Your world spread coolly out through distance seen
Not clasped, up close and muggy to you tight
Like mine, nor lost when space drops in between.
We move through different rooms. They say yours fills
Like glass, with some diffuse transparency,
Intangible except when color spills
Across the gap yet keeps your privacy.

And still in dark your distance holds.
You can't collapse the open reach and spread
To be wrapped up like me with cotton folds
The room drawn small around you in the bed.
But what if touch could see? Could bring
In one collective sweep this place to mind?
All things would rush against my skin and fling
No heat or texture just the airy blind.

Caress of wood, the fabric's droop, and fleet
Of dust. Each cornered, blunt, or jagged shape
And dreg of space would rain, a single sheet
Of tactile sense like vision's steady drape.

I'd feel you flush, your body's breadth and height,
Upon my length. I'd know at once this room.

And you inside the room. Your every sleight
Of hand and careless gesture I'd consume.

Instead, I sit before your gaze, submit
To some ubiquitous touch, and let you trace
My frame, envelop me. So please admit
The barest press of fingers to your face.

Amy Alznauer lives in Chicago where she teaches mathematics at DePaul University. Her work also appears in Creative Nonfiction, River Teeth, *and the* Bellingham Review. *She is the winner of the 2005 Annie Dillard Award for Creative Nonfiction.*

Celebration On Hold
Judith Rieder Squier

I get the feeling the day of my birth was not a celebration. No one ever said, but I have a hunch my birth announcement had an invisible PS that everyone could see, "In lieu of balloons, bring a hankie."

My midnight arrival was like a cold shower to the unsuspecting obstetrician. With no prepared speech for such a tragedy he blurted out "Your daughter is going to live I am sorry to say." That's what my dad recollects. Mom remembers that she waited three days before I was brought to her. Expecting the worst, she was surprised to find me "capable, not a vegetable" as I turned over in the nurse's nervous arms. "And your big brown eyes," mom swears, "jumped out and wrapped themselves around my heart."

Leaving Geneva Hospital that cold day in March, no pink blanket could hide the fact that I had a severe birth defect—a webbed left hand and two undeveloped legs with no thighs or knees and a total of five, instead of ten toes. (Proximal femoral focal deficiency was later attached to the hospital record.)

Mom and Dad say my 5 lb. 6 oz. incomplete body seemed light in contrast to the unending questions weighing heavy on their broken hearts: Is our baby going to die? Can we take care of her? If she lives, is she educable? Will she ever enjoy life?

Too busy to stay stuck on the questions, my family dug in their heels. Changing diaper after diaper on a baby with webbed feet cured the initial shock. People's dead silence in place of "What a beautiful baby" made mom madder than a hornet, but ceased being a surprise. Tears, hard work, laughter, faith, failure and success filled the years ahead.

Countless doctors' appointments, operations, trips to the brace man and eventual placement in special education (plus the usual stuff called "growing-up") filled each week to the fullest. But the life-changing event we had all held our breaths for, came when I was ten. At Shriner's Hospital in Chicago I underwent corrective surgery and traded my deformed footies for stumps and my metal stilts for artificial limbs. Standing tall for the first time in my life, my willow legs and I walked the hospital corridor the day I was discharged.

My legs and I entered domains no one ever dreamed possible: a military ball, driving a car, summer jobs at a camp, college and a sorority filled and thrilled my adolescent years. And the prize after six years at the University of Illinois was a Master's Degree in Speech Pathology, the same month I received my "MRS" Degree and became Mrs. David Squier.

These milestones became midget-size compared to the births of my three daughters. God more than compensated for everything I had missed times three. Vicariously, I have walked, run, jumped rope, rollerbladed and played soccer. Sitting at Emily's piano recital, watching her nimble ten fingers make "El Shaddai" dance on the keyboard, I have wondered if the concert auditorium would shake as shivers of celebration danced up and down my spine. And I've gloried in the back flips and front walk-overs as Betsy's and Naphtalie's limber legs have carried me, their mom, the length of the gymnasium.

Somewhere in the journey, at different times for each of us, the hundreds of family and friends touched by my disability exchanged the no-longer-needed hankies for helium balloons. Unbeknownst to us, God had made my life a celebration. Together we had learned that disability is a potential delivery room for the extraordinary, the unprecedented and the inconceivable.

Judy Rieder Squier resides in southern Oregon with her husband of thirty-eight years, David. Her careers have been in speech pathology, the mothering of three daughters, public speaking, and freelance writing. Her messages overflow with gratitude to a God who pulls off the impossible. Check out her website at www.squierfamily.net and contact her at judyann777@aol.com.

Catching Kate
Suzanne Robitaille

They put me on the bottom of the pyramid. They tell me to stand there and wait for Kate, our expert flier, to drop. But I never feel her weight in my arms. Instead, a whisper, a nod, gives her courage to flip and fall, knowing she will be caught by them, not me.

It is my first year on the team, as a sophomore at Bishop Morton High School. We are a mighty team and win prizes and ribbons everywhere we go. We beat the other Catholic squads and the chain-smoking fishermen's daughters at the public schools, too. We place first in the regionals, which earns us a spot in the nationals, down in Myrtle Beach. For this we train rigorously with Coach Julie, who makes us practice our Russian splits for forty-five minutes each day, followed by sit-ups and laps around the track.

I am a strong girl, five-foot-five, probably 120 pounds. My Irish face lends me a clean and youthful look, and I have been streaking my hair with Henna since junior high. I am not an athlete, but I am not lots of things that most sophomores are. I like libraries, newspapers, and politics. I hate music, movies, and the McDonald's drive-thru.

I haven't been able to hear since I was four years old. I attended a school for the deaf, but ultimately my mother mainstreamed me. It was she who invited my neighbor, Karena, to play with me one Saturday afternoon when I was eight. The same age as me, Karena was already a pointe dancer and an extra in the Boston production of "The Nutcracker." She has professional shots taken of her in her leotard and we had one taped to our refrigerator, her small square teeth displaying thin lips glossed with Vaseline, her brown hair wrapped tightly in a bun twirled with baby's breath.

That day she brought over an Olivia Newton-John tape and we play it on my boom box. I can't hear the words or the tempo, and besides, I have no interest in music. I desperately want Karena to go home so I can return to my pile of library books. Karena is implicitly bored with my company. She stands up and with a shake of her hips, starts dancing to Olivia's hit song, "Physical," with her lithe body. She fans her hands up and over her head and plunges forward, and then kicks her leg up so her pink knee warmers almost touch her cheek. I am drawn to these liberating moves, which seem to impart a level of maturity that I haven't reached.

Over the next several hours in my bedroom, Karena teaches me an entire dance routine. In front of an imaginary audience, I count the spaces between the hard beats—which I can vaguely make out if the volume on the boom box is all the way up. Like the couth cabaret dancers I once saw on a field trip in Chicago at the Shubert, we grind, pout, cascade, and catwalk across my bedroom carpet over and over again until I have memorized the three-minute number and Karena has gone from being a lukewarm playmate to a peerless authority on jazz, and who, by a pure result of being stuck at my house, has summoned in me a rhapsodic appreciation for music. There, in my very bedroom, I discover that a song that I may not be able to hear can instead be broken down into beats, spaces and a sequential rhythmic order from start to finish. By mastering the choreography, no one can tell I can't hear the music.

Twice weekly classes for five years with my mother's encouragement help me to become a proficient jazz dancer. I learn to jazz square, cake walk, mess around, figure 8, hinge, pitch, release, freeze!, shiver, and snake. It is my mother who puts the idea in my head to try out for the cheerleading squad when I enter Bishop Morton High School, calling it a perfect accompaniment to my flexibility and groove, on what is her brazen wish that I will shake off my seriousness and become one of those cute, peppy girls with the rolled socks and bangles. And perhaps shake off my deafness, too, for my own benefit.

I make the cut on the varsity squad and begin practicing cheers with eleven other teenagers who snatch trophies with as much detachment as a pack of well-fed alley cats. The ruling cheerleaders, seniors mostly, grant access to their circle based first on looks and second on talent. They don't like my nasally voice, or how I refuse to wear my hair in braids so as not to show my hearing aid. I can't hear on the telephone, and the social cavalcade skips my house. My balance is so damaged by the meningitis that my splits are never as graceful, my cartwheels are never as perfect, and when I miss verbal cues, I'm out of sync and the accord of a cheer is ruined. And what hurts most is when we form pyramids, the other cheerleaders won't let me catch Kate, our top flier who shows her athletic prowess with giant leaps and a long ponytail suspended in the air. Though I'm a solid performer and dancer, Kate is off limits to me.

Thanks to Coach Julie, we win most of the competitions we enter. With enough practice, my deafness is manageable, in the sense that I hide it well enough. I memorize the routines and play the music close enough to my ear to at least make out the bass and deeper frequencies. Inside, I'm alone. Outside,

I'm an outcast. I grin and bear it.

Until the day of the national competition down in Myrtle Beach, in April of 1990. It is our turn. The music starts, Coach Julie nods. I count eight beats, jump up from a crouched position and moonwalk with my team across the squeaky gymnasium floor. Another eight counts, then a tumble with extra smiles, please! We form a triple line for our solitary splits. Four beats, then the pyramid-building begins. Coach Julie designed our twelve-person pyramid as a Byzantine contraption, formed by two triple-half extensions and two Liberties on either side, then switching to a triple hitch, which calls for five smaller girls, the fliers, climbing onto the shoulders of me and six other base girls.

Kate, the center fly, is popped into a double twist, but instead of twirling, she kicks another base girl in the face with her foot. This dismantles our pyramid with Kate still somewhere in mid-air. I catch her, alone. She lands with a thud on my chest, and I hit the ground, my wrist red-hot and stinging. The judges watch silently, wondering if we can recover. Coach Julie runs over with a horrified look on her face. The dance tape is stopped. I stop counting beats.

We are all sour at our loss that day. My wrist is sprained and wrapped in tattered gauze. What hurts more is how it took a toppling, and a bruising in a million places, to prove my competence. The team shows some gratitude, but I can hardly digest it.

The cheerleaders' web of perfection was imperfect that day. Humanity is frail and nature is uncompromising, but they don't learn this until later in life. They wanted a championship, they got an embarrassment. They expected a trophy, but got me instead. In catching Kate, I caught myself. You take what you can get.

Suzanne Robitaille is a former journalist who has worked at The Wall Street Journal *and* BusinessWeek Online, *where she wrote the Assistive Technology column. She lost her hearing at age four to meningitis and received a cochlear implant in 2002, which enabled her to hear on the telephone for the first time. Suzanne is an executive speechwriter at American Express. She resides in New York City.*

An Astronaut on Earth
Paul Kahn

By the fall of 1987 I could no longer breathe on my own and was facing death from asphyxiation. This was the grim endpoint of a long decline caused by my centronuclear myopathy, a congenital, progressive neuromuscular disability.

For many years I had been getting ventilation at night from a positive pressure respirator that fed air to me through a lip-sealed mouthpiece. During the day, although limited by the need to use a motorized wheelchair, I was independent enough to do things that mattered to me, such as working as a counselor, making art and socializing. But gradually, as my breathing muscles weakened, I began to require more respiratory assistance during the day. I started using oxygen from a canister. Then came the need for the respirator during an hour in the late afternoon. One hour became insufficient, and inexorably I progressed to extended and repeated intervals on the respirator throughout the day. Even so, I was always tired. Any exercise, mental or physical, exhausted me and required great willpower to perform. I lost weight because I didn't have the energy to eat. My life was measured and restricted by the few hours of relative comfort I experienced before cyanosis forced me to return to the respirator.

I knew I could not continue that way. So, in November, fearful and desperate, I had myself admitted to the respiratory care center of a large Boston hospital. There I underwent a tracheotomy and became permanently dependent on a ventilator. My physical and psychological recovery from this life-changing event formed one of the most frightening, difficult and yet rewarding adventures of my life. It taught me a great deal about the internal and external resources that enable people to cope with traumatic change. And, it provided me with valuable insights about self-determination and the ability of the psyche to incorporate and adapt to new realities.

I had suffered so long with my deteriorating health because I was afraid both of the operation and the outcome. As long as I can recall, I have been deeply distrustful of other people, while ironically having to depend on them for my basic needs. The struggle to achieve some measure of self-reliance has been central to my life. To lie unconscious on the operating table and let masked strangers hold my life in their latex-gloved hands seemed the antithesis of independence. I was also afraid of how the operation might change the quality of my life. Being completely dependent on a ventilator, would I always feel anxious about it breaking down? Would I ever again be able to enjoy the peace of solitude, or would I always need to have someone hovering around me to provide emergency aid? Would other people be frightened or repulsed by my strange accouterments of tubes and hardware? In particular, how would my new girlfriend Ruth feel? Would she continue to find me attractive? And how would I feel about myself? Being so intimately, so inextricably joined to a machine, would I feel less human, like a robot instead of a flesh-and-blood man? The image came to me of a space-walking astronaut, tethered by a fragile umbilical line to his capsule. Never could he forget how deadly was the void in which he floated, how without his clumsy, high-tech gadgetry he would die. I imagined seeing the strain of constant fear on his helmeted face. I wondered: would I be an astronaut on earth?

The surgery consisted of making an opening at the base of my throat into my trachea and inserting a curved, plastic tracheostomy tube, to which a volume ventilator was then attached. All went well, and the next morning Ruth and my parents were amazed to find me sitting up in my wheelchair, looking pinker and more energized than they had seen me in a very long time.

However, there were unanticipated delays in my progress toward full recovery. Two disheartening problems were my inability to talk or eat for several weeks after the surgery. Both eventually resolved, but I suffered intense anxiety until they did. I remember particularly well getting a pass from the hospital on Thanksgiving, going to my parents' home, and having to sit and watch them and Ruth dine on turkey, stuffing and all the usual—but to me forbidden—holiday delights. It was torture, and, in my jealousy, I cheated just a bit by dipping my finger into the gravy and tasting it.

I began to eat again just in time to celebrate Ruth and my sixth month anniversary of going together. She brought to the hospital a special meal she had purchased at a gourmet shop. We had lasagna, wine, and chocolate truffles for dessert. There was much to celebrate—the return of my health, the survival of our relationship—and yet much to feel anxious about. We wondered: what would life be like at home with the ventilator, outside the security of the hospital?

Much of my stay was devoted to getting ready for that transition. I realized that to regain my independence and feel comfortable in my apartment again I would have to understand my new care needs and be able to teach them to my attendants. Also, Ruth and I knew that, if we were to have any privacy, she would have to learn everything, too. I wanted badly to be in charge of my life again.

Intensely motivated, I applied myself, and the learning posed no great difficulties. In fact, I found some enjoyment in acquiring new skills, and the process gave a focus to my days: I was working on going home. And I could hardly wait to leave. The long hospitalization had been proving very stressful. One-half of a small, bare room was an impoverished environment to live in. I brought in books, games, art supplies and writing materials, anything I thought would keep my mind active, but still I struggled to feel psychologically alive.

Probably the greatest stress of being in the hospital was the disruption of my relationship with Ruth. When I was admitted we had been going together for less than five months and were still in the first flush of wonder and pleasure at our intimacy. To be thrust into an environment that afforded us no privacy, no chance to escape from the compelling but abnormal drama of my recovery, seemed a great loss. We railed and grieved, but eventually came to understand that the hospitalization was not an interruption in our relationship but a continuation of it. Once we had accepted that, we could appreciate the richness of our situation—my progress toward health, the sweetness of our kisses when that was all we could give each other, the support of our families and friends. We came to realize that wherever we were together could be our home. That realization was the first lesson of the tracheotomy, the first answer to the questions I had asked myself about what the quality of my life would be. The quality would depend on me, on my attitude, not on my physical baggage or surroundings.

I entered the hospital on November 3, and forty-three days later on December 15 I was discharged. The chief resident's parting words to me were, "Congratulations on your new marriage to the ventilator. I'm sure that with your creativity you'll make the relationship work." I hoped so, but at that point he had more faith in me than I had in myself. My attendant Jeff loaded my van with my equipment and belongings, and I went out into the crisp late autumn morning, rejoicing about being a survivor. But on the way home, anxiety overtook me. I became afraid that the ventilator hose might disconnect from the tracheostomy tube, interrupting the flow of air on which I depended. Could I reattach the tube by myself? Could Jeff stop the van on the turnpike to help me? And how long would I be able to breathe on my own, if I had to? I didn't know the answers to any of these questions, so I held myself stiffly and prayed that the bouncing of the van would not shake anything loose. We got home without mishap and were met by therapists from my home care company, who had come to bring additional supplies, help me organize storage and equipment space and clarify their services. I was glad of their competent presence and, when they left, again felt a dread. "What now?" I thought. Now I had to be the resident expert.

Gradually, my fears about equipment failure dissipated. With the ungrateful sarcasm we sometimes direct towards the people and things on which we are dependent, I called my ventilator a pretentious and over-priced air compressor. But I developed a grudging respect for its intelligence, efficiency and reliability. Soon I felt quite safe being alone at home.

Away from home I always had to keep a manual ventilating device called an ambu bag with me for emergency use. I also always had to travel with other supplies, such as a portable suction machine and suction catheters. At first I worried that I would forget to take these necessities with me or forget to reorder supplies and run out. But stocking my travel bag and keeping up supplies eventually became an automatic rhythm. I also became adept at troubleshooting minor problems when they did occur, such as a cracked air filter or a loose connection in the circuitry. So, while I learned to trust my equipment, I also learned to trust myself. And that was the second lesson of the tracheotomy—the knowledge that I could be more mature than I had previously thought. I could be responsible for my complex needs, and I could tolerate the degree of risk that was unavoidable, if I wanted to live a full life.

When I first started going back into the world, I felt very conspicuous with the tracheostomy tube and ventilator. The experience was like becoming disabled all over again. A lifetime of using a wheelchair had accustomed me to stares and the quick, uncomfortable turning away of eyes. But more recently improved access had made people with disabilities less of a rarity in public and had decreased unwanted attention. But disabled people with ventilators were still a minority within a minority. I expected the world to greet me with a renewed onslaught of pity and fear, the old there-but-for-the-grace-of-God syndrome reborn in all its alienating force. Part of me wanted to avoid this confrontation and keep to the security of home. But I had struggled through the ordeal of the tracheotomy in order to have a fuller life, not a more restricted one, so I ventured out.

Whether my predictions were accurate or not, I can't say. It's hard to judge what strangers really feel. But I'm sure that my tracheotomy mattered very little to the significant people in my life. When I went back to my work as a psychological counselor, my patients were simply glad that I was again able to attend to their problems. With the self-centeredness to which therapy gives complete permission, they were primarily concerned with how my condition might impact them. Once reassured that I was healthy and not going to die or leave them again, they largely ignored my new equipment. My colleagues were for the most part politely disinterested, a lack of reaction that troubled me. I had, after all, gone through hell and back. So, I was grateful to those who wanted to hear my story. A few months after my tracheotomy I happened to meet an old friend, whom I had not seen for several years. She greeted me warmly and with great naturalness pointed to my ventilator. "That's new, isn't it?" she asked. I told her what had happened, and when I was finished she smiled and said, "It must have worked, because you look great. I'm glad for you." I thanked her for the compliment but was even more pleased by how comfortable she had made me feel.

The truth was that the tracheotomy had deeply upset my sense of identity. My bodily integrity felt violated, my fetal helplessness seemed confirmed. I needed to heal myself and feel whole again. I soon learned that the ways of self-healing I had used before still worked for me. This was the third lesson—I was still essentially the same person, even though physically I had changed.

One of my most important ways of self-healing was artistic expression. By giving visual or written form to my feelings, I have always felt able, through some sympathetic magic, to recreate myself. I began putting this process to work while I was still in the hospital. The idea occurred to me of creating a mural to express the drama we were going through. My inspiration was Matisse, who in his old age was confined to bed and too arthritic to handle a paintbrush. So, he created collages by cutting shapes out of colored paper and directing his assistants where to place them on the wall in front of him. I modified his example by deciding that, instead of keeping autocratic control, I would let Ruth and my attendants be artistic partners and contribute to the design. That seemed only fair, since they were partners in my ordeal as well.

We began by bringing in a supply of construction paper, scissors, tape and glue and then covering most of one wall of my room with a large sheet of heavy, white paper. I made a sketch of the area and divided it into three sections. The left I labeled "sickness," the center "recovery" and the right "health." Together they would tell my story. "Sickness" we decided should be dark, cramped, sad and weak. "Recovery" would be agitated, hopeful and uncertain. And "health" must be bright, expansive, happy, strong and free. We went to work, and the blank wall slowly began to fill up with the shapes and colors of our imaginations.

The progress of the mural paralleled my progress and was a powerful way of externalizing my tensions and dissipating some of their force. When I returned home, I continued to explore my experience in more finished work. The first painting I completed I called "Steppenwolf," after the novel by Hermann Hesse.

The theme of the novel, the divided soul, seemed to mirror my own inner tensions and confusions. I was torn between rejoicing and regret. The rational adult in me knew to count his blessings of health, but the undisciplined child railed against the cost to his freedom and resented the burden of limitations and responsibilities. I wavered between hope and dread. I might have life now, but death had come so close I could never feel completely safe again. And I still did not know which to celebrate—the fury of my will to survive or the abeyance of my will and acceptance of the suffering that made survival possible. In the painting, these dualities were represented by the man and the wolf. By integrating these figures within a balanced, circular composition, I found a symbolic, ritualistic way of integrating and transcending my psychological conflicts.

Vital as this self-healing was to my emotional recovery, it was matched, if not surpassed, in importance by Ruth's love. I had feared that the ordeal of the tracheotomy would be too steep a price for her to want to pay for being involved with me and that my newly mechanized body would repel her. Neither of these fears proved true. While I was in the hospital she remained connected and committed, going through the changes along with me. Her frequent visits were the happiest, most eagerly anticipated events of my days. Though I felt torn by the conflicting claims of the brave adult and the rebellious child in me, Ruth accepted and loved both. She used to hold me and tell me it was okay to cry and rage. I didn't have to prove myself to her. By embracing all of me she helped me realize that I was still worthwhile. Attaining this knowledge was the fourth and most important lesson.

One year after my surgery, Ruth and I were married. In the ceremony, we remembered the poignant lessons of adjustment. "Only a little over a year ago I was very ill," I told our family and friends, "and the future seemed rapidly to be closing in on me. Now it has miraculously opened again. I have my health and my dear love, Ruth, one to enjoy it with." Ruth, in her turn, told our guests how my tracheostomy had helped her understand the symbolism of the "chuppa" in the Jewish marriage ceremony. "Our 'chuppa'—our home—is always with us," she said, "whether it be a two-bedroom apartment or one-half of a crowded hospital room."

We ended our ceremony with the beautiful Shaker hymn, "Simple Gifts." "'Tis a gift to be simple, home 'tis a gift to be free," we all sang together. Reflecting on the year just passed, I thought that, of course, life was far from simple. It was full of complicated trials and suffering. Yet, I also believed that one might even so be free—free of despair, free to enjoy love, creativity and the panoply of sensations that constitute being alive.

To this day my life remains rich. My disability has continued to progress, but mechanical ventilation has maintained my vitality. I still have energy to work, create and enjoy my marriage. And from time to time I still envision that space-walking astronaut who symbolized my apprehensions. But now that image has a different quality. Fear still sometimes flickers across his face, but more often it is lit by expressions of awe and delight at the wonderful adventure he is privileged to have. Like him, my adventure, my life, goes on, and I have many more reasons to be glad than sorry.

Paul Kahn, M.Ed., is a playwright, poet, essayist, and editor. He has received grants from the Massachusetts Cultural Council, the Newton Cultural Council ,and the Christopher Reeve Paralysis Foundation. He has won awards from the Massachusetts Rehabilitation Commission, the Muscular Dystrophy Association, and his alma mater Boston University.

Catch-22 Blues
Robert Seelenfreund

It's not easy to detect Parkinson's disease. It worms its way into your life slowly, much like a bad relationship does. It builds up one small step at a time, you don't focus on the big picture, and then one day you wake up and say to yourself. Holy shit, why didn't I notice this before?

Even with that caveat it seems ludicrous that a disease overtook my body and I failed to notice the invasion. I had clearly been in what the twelve-steppers call a state of denial. For well over a year, I had been oblivious to the fact that my body had gone almost completely haywire. In my defense, I was a career public defender, and along with having defended countless criminals came a recurring fantasy that I, myself, was on trial for some hideous offense. I would offer as proof my reasonable, if faulty, assumption that Parkinson's disease was strictly for old people. It was August, 1996, two years before Michael J. Fox went public. And I was only forty-three years old.

Yes, I would admit on cross-examination that I had seen Muhammed Ali's hands shaking wildly at the opening ceremonies of the Olympics that summer. And yes, I did note the similarity: my hand shook sporadically, if not repeatedly, while I was in court. It was always the left hand, and when I wasn't hiding it from myself, I hid it under the counsel table. But our now-aging former world champion had received a million blows to the head. While I had inflicted and received verbal blows galore, I had not been in a fistfight since junior high school. And finally, my once robust, never-sick-a-day-in-his-life father had recently succumbed to the ravages of stomach cancer. It was just stress. That had become my mantra.

I developed an expertise in creating alternative explanations for my body's failure to perform the most basic tasks. The shirts that I found nearly impossible to button were poorly manufactured. Because I struggled mightily to open a jar of maple syrup, I tried to convince Emily that cereal was a more nutritious breakfast than waffles. Much more frightening than this growing inability to perform deft tasks with my hands were the mysterious lane changes that occurred on the highway. While driving to and from work I would suddenly notice I had drifted into the left lane. I realized something was wrong and resolved to bring the Honda for a checkup. But I never quite remembered to do so. Other problems surfaced while I was driving. Motorists driving behind me on the Garden State Parkway honked furiously while I took nearly forever to complete the complicated tasks of gathering up the coins, opening the window and throwing them into the baskets at the tollbooths. It did not occur to me that I was experiencing a diminution of my fine motor skills; I merely made a mental note about increased road rage.

My life began to resemble a protracted episode of *The Twilight Zone*. It, the weird strangeness that was invading my life, came to visit me in court, where I stumbled my way through trials. Things got worse. Walking became problematic. My gait was off. I began to notice I was taking shorter steps. This method of ambulating did not so much resemble walking as it did hobbling along. I began to move like the less than sprightly senior citizens that hung around the town pool. My whole feeling of balance was off kilter; I fell off a bicycle for no apparent reason. I was suffering from terminal awkwardness, as if I was back at a junior high school dance. Only now I was not just afraid of girls, but of life itself.

These symptoms presented a more daunting challenge to rationalize. I convinced myself that these difficulties were nothing more than an intense case of creeping middle-aged sloth. I just needed to get back in shape. Despite my basic problem with movement, I turned into a mean-spirited redneck drill sergeant and forced myself to exercise. I tried to jog but as time went by I simply couldn't do it. So I switched to fast walking, but my toes would curl up and my legs would cramp right in the middle of a workout.

While my body betrayed me in a myriad of ways, I watched my father slowly die from cancer. I latched onto that sad experience as an explanation for all the oddball occurrences that had engulfed me; it became the ace-in-the-hole of my denial. One night I fell in the shower and the veil of denial was finally pierced. I made an appointment with a neurologist.

I also began rereading *Catch 22*. It was more than a mere novel to me; it was the treasured book of my youth that helped me cope with the death of my brother. As an adult it helped me cope with the news that our daughter was born with a severe bone disorder. I regarded it with a reverence usually reserved for the Holy Bible; I quoted passages from my Good Book about as often as preachers did from theirs. When things went to hell, I went to Heller.

Armored up to my teeth in absurdity, I went to the neurologist's office. After my terse recital of symptoms the doctor examined me. It was remarkably quick. Move this finger. Touch your nose. Reach out to my shoulder. Snap your fingers. Faster, if you can. Let me see you walk down the hall. Then back to the fingers. Touch your pointer finger to your thumb. Keep doing it. Now do that with the other hand.

"Now let's see you smile."

I grimly complied. Did this mean I was about to suffer through an inspirational speech on the value of a positive attitude? No, as it turned out; he was just testing my facial muscles.

"I take it that you are aware of Parkinson's disease, and what its symptoms are. And I'm sure that you've thought about Parkinson's.

I had not thought about it, and didn't want to think about it now. What I did think about was the episode in *Catch 22* when Major Sanderson, the Army psychiatrist, told Yossarian that his personality was "split right down the middle."

"'I'm not saying that to be cruel and insulting,' he continued with cruel and insulting delight. 'I'm not saying it because I hate you and want revenge. I'm not saying it because you rejected me and hurt my feelings terribly. No, I'm a man of medicine and I'm being coldly objective. I have very bad news for you. Are you man enough to take it?'

'God, no!' screamed Yossarian. 'I'll go right to pieces.'

Major Sanderson flew instantly into a rage. 'Can't you even do one thing right?'"

I returned from my reverie and listened to the doctor say that medicine would help. I took the prescription from Dr. Stein and went home.

The good news was that Parkinson's was not fatal. It could make your body go whacko in a hundred different ways and rob you of your dignity. But it supposedly couldn't kill you. I could therefore continue to emulate Yossarian, whose goal was "to live forever or die in the attempt." The hard question I asked myself was not when would I die, but how would I live?

Parky and I may be companions for life so we have learned to live with each other. (It now seems downright silly to have referred to my disease as "the enemy.") As in any relationship there are, of course, things about him I don't like. Parky often insists on taking a mid-day nap even if I need to get things done. His refusal to allow me to write legibly is annoying and I've become dependent on computers to accommodate him. Parky demands my attention at the most inconvenient times. Just as I'm getting into my rhythm on a treadmill Parky will make my toes curl up. Or cramp up my left leg. Sometimes I can manage the situation by lowering the speed of the machine; usually I have to stop. I've talked to him about this until I'm blue in the face. He claims to understand how much it means to me to stay in shape, but on this issue he is plain old stubborn. He simply gets bored with repetitive movements and is not going to change; I just have to accept that rigidity is part of Parky's personality.

It's not always clear to me why Parky is so demanding. He certainly doesn't suffer from a lack of attention. I do plenty for him. I feed Parky pills all day long, and do boring stretching exercises every morning. I gave up coffee and soda, and rarely consume alcohol. Because he seems convinced that acupuncture is beneficial, I even allow needles to be inserted all over my body. And I have explored New Age affirmation exercises to teach me how to get along with a difficult partner. Some of them seem pretty silly—I know a lot of people, including many of my own friends, would condescendingly sneer at my using these kind of self-help techniques—but I find others to be surprisingly effective in bringing about a change in both attitude and behavior. As the old saying goes: Any port in a storm.

My relationship with Parky may seem one sided to an outsider. But I've gained quite a lot from him, too. Parky has taught me that going through life at a slower pace offers its own rewards. He has shown me the wisdom of living in the present, and that has dramatically improved my capacity to enjoy right now. I used to spend much of my time plagued by the past, or anxious about the future. What wasted energy!

It helps that we share common interests; I am thrilled to death that Parky loves to hike as much as I do. He feels better after a long day on the trail. It's true that he prefers a much slower pace than I do. But this is more than compensated for by his insistence that on hiking days we rise at 5:00 a.m., which allows us adequate time to reach distant summits and still return before sunset. While visiting my cousin, Marty Eisenberg, a college professor who spends as much time as he possibly can in his Colorado mountain house, we were able to reach the summit of three 14,000 foot mountains!

Before Parky came into my life I lacked the discipline to rise before the sun and drive off in the groggy pre-dawn darkness. Now we regularly enjoy the beauty and stillness of the woods at dawn, a precious time during which the world slowly wakes up and tranquility is available with every step. After a rocky start, Parky and I have become quite compatible. The question naturally arises: How long will the honeymoon last? Many advanced Parkinsonians use exactly that phrase to describe the five-to-ten year period after their diagnosis when the Sinemet works so effectively. The real crunch comes later, they report, when the dosage level becomes so high that the side effects are often worse than the symptoms. Dyskinesia can occur so frequently during sleep that bed partners, tired of being kicked, depart for safer quarters. Then the medicine itself ceases to be so terrific at alleviating symptoms and you experience the dreaded "on-off" effect: One moment you're fine, and then suddenly you're frozen and can't move at all until the next dose takes effect. My Parkinsonian cousins say that under those conditions walking to the nearby grocery store to buy a quart of milk can easily degenerate into an unwanted adventure, if not a fiasco.

Unfortunately, the future has arrived. The above assessment is accurate, and the progression of Parkinson's seems beyond my capabilities to stop. The symptoms vary like weather in the mountains. I walk well for an hour; later that day, I can hardly make it to the bathroom. At night I often use a walker.

What about making a living? I am still a public defender but not in the courtroom. I am no less intelligent than I was fifteen years ago, but trial lawyers have to be able to think quickly and make rapid decisions. There are many ways to be an ineffective lawyer but a late objection is one of the worst. Not only have you failed to stop the testimony from being heard by the jury, but you've also highlighted it. That was just one of the many examples that made me realize it was time to move on. Luckily for me, my office has an appellate unit and I can still write a mean brief.

Can I still hike? Yes and no. Climbing mountains in Colorado is a memory. A short jaunt is fine but here's a catch of my own: Given that loss of balance is an issue, I have given up hiking alone. Yet, as my pace has deteriorated to that of the lowly turtle, it's become a bit much to expect my hiking partners to join me. They are not living their lives in slow motion.

I came to see my disease as a price my body paid for having been at the mercy of my rage and other warring emotions for so many years. It was not easy to face this truth, but it did represent a turning point in my life. And if I could "make" myself sick, was it also then possible to make myself better? It's easy to advocate clichés about acceptance of one's condition and banishing negativity during the first stages of the disease. It's like winning a game against the j.v.; let's hold the excitement until we see how we fare against the varsity. Outside of novels and movies, growth-when it occurs at all-happens slowly, incrementally, and with lots of setbacks. And in my journey, at least, my fears, rage, and paralyzing anxieties did not disappear (wouldn't that be nice?) but have accompanied me every step of the way. My feelings toward my bundle of negative emotions matched what Mr. Bennet felt about his wife's "poor nerves" in *Pride and Prejudice:* "You mistake me, my dear. I have a high respect for your nerves. They are my old friends. I have heard you mention them with consideration these twenty years at least."

Joseph Heller died in 1999, but that hasn't stopped me from being inspired by *Catch 22.* Like a Talmudist who sees new meanings with each rereading of sacred religious texts, I derive new perspectives from familiar passages. I used to applaud Yossarian's boast to Lieutenant Scheisskopf's wife that he could, "name two things to be miserable about for every one you can name to be thankful for." But now, grappling daily with logistics that often make life seem like an endless obstacle course, I try very hard to side with the first speaker in the above characters' argument:

> *Be thankful you're healthy.*
> *Be bitter you're not going to stay that way.*
> *Be glad you're even alive.*
> *Be furious you're going to die.*
> *Things could be much worse, she cried.*
> *They could be one hell of a lot better, he answered heatedly.*

Has all this qualified as an epiphany? I wouldn't know one of those if it slapped me in the face. It doesn't come in a box, gift-wrapped like a certificate from Macy's. But I have liberated my creativity from its captivity and finish manuscripts, a claim I couldn't make in my pre-Parkinson's life.

I remain flexible about the future. I take substantial number of pills every day. The pharmaceutical giants know there are billions of dollars to be made by developing a cure for this disease; its researchers are working feverishly to insure that their company is first and can grab the patent. Given all the medical miracles that occurred in the last century, it does not seem unreasonable to expect that a drug will be invented that can rouse up the millions of little dopamine cells from their inhospitable slumber. And, if not? I'll be shuffling off, if not to Buffalo, then to wherever I have to go. Don't hold me to a time, but get there I will.

Robert Seelenfreund is a lawyer who lives with his wife and two daughters in West Orange, New Jersey.

Confessions of a Disabled Swimmer
Robert S. Kahan

I would like to tell you about one day in summer camp when I was twelve years old and swam across a lake in a race, because it was a turning point in my lifelong struggle to overcome disability. In doing so I want to emphasize two aspects of disability that are not readily apparent:

1. Being disabled is not entirely bad. In fact, there are certain advantages in disability that have made my life better than it would have been otherwise.

2. These positive attributes of disability can be used to overcome its disadvantages.

Please don't jump to conclusions. I am not about to tell you that I have achieved "Wisdom Through Suffering." I have nothing good to say about suffering. Like so many other handicapped people, I am all too familiar with pain, fatigue, clumsiness, humiliation, depression, self-loathing, etc. None of that has taught me much I care to remember.

Nor am I going to argue that disability can be overcome by denying its shortcomings, as one well-meaning doctor suggested when he quoted an old proverb: "Remember, the body is a useless appendage to the mind." Oh, how I wish that were true, but it isn't. In spite of what Plato argued, that we have a "higher" self and a "lower" self, a mind/body dichotomy, we are all of a piece. Our thoughts, feelings, and physical state are inextricably interwoven. In other words, you cannot make your handicap disappear by wishing it weren't so.

For clarity's sake, allow me to say just what my disability is before going on. I have an Erb's Palsy—impaired use of my left arm, hand and shoulder—caused by severe damage to the nerves controlling those parts of my body. The damage occurred at birth. I was in a breech position, stuck inside my mother, and was rotated with forceps to get me out. In doing so, the obstetrician, who had grabbed my head and left side with his forceps, exerted too much force and almost pulled me apart. I've tried to picture the scene several times: my mother in prolonged labor and distress, doing all the right things, but nothing happening; a worried doctor under pressure to do something before matters got worse; and me, almost eleven pounds, feeling the grip of cold steel and what must have been incredible pain. Years later, my father, who sometimes tried to make light of my condition to bolster my morale, said, "You were born ass-backwards."

I did not move for the first year of my life. Literally. Every two hours, night and day, one of my parents changed my position and wiggled my arms and legs. The fear was that, otherwise, I would "freeze" and never move. My mother and father were fond of recalling the day I began moving on my own, somewhere near my first birthday, and the tears and celebration that followed.

My first movements were signals to the doctors that I was ready to begin a serious rehabilitation program. This included exercises designed to give me not only mobility, but also the strength I lacked. Rehabilitation specialists today speak of such training as "range of motion" exercises. In my case that largely consisted of spending hours every week for the next decade in a swimming pool. I literally learned to swim before I learned to walk. Once again, that meant extraordinary commitment from my parents who, until I could manage on my own, had to take me to the water, get in it with me, and give me swimming lessons.

I've asked my mother and father about this intensive care they provided in my first decade of childhood and how they really felt about it. After all, there they were, a young couple anticipating their first child and the joys of parenthood—and they got me. What were the doubts and fears they experienced in my first year when, inert, I kept them from a full night's sleep and offered none of the usual infant delights in return? And what must they have wondered about my mental development? Would it be permanently arrested, too? I gave them no clues, no solace, in this regard during my first year. Just silence. Entropy.

Neither of my parents ever expressed resentment or anger about their disappointment and the extraordinary amount of time, energy and money required for my rehabilitation. If they did feel misgivings, some sense of being cheated, they did not complain or hold me responsible for all of the costs that my condition brought them. They accepted their lot and met their unexpected, undeserved responsibilities with unstinted love.

The first bit of advice I offer on overcoming disability, then, is to have parents who are saints. I took this for granted when I was a boy and was not disappointed. Later, especially after I became a father, I learned that sainthood was a status that had to be earned through sacrifice and without reluctance.

So, on that afternoon at camp as I crouched on the dock, poised to dive into the lake along with a dozen other boys awaiting the signal to begin racing to the far shore, I bore a secret: I had been in training for this event most of my life. In the course of my rehabilitation, in that decade of swimming therapy begun in infancy, those years of learning to move, I had developed into a boy employing a smooth Australian crawl who regularly did thirty laps in a fifty-meter pool. As I looked at the far shore of the lake, the finish line some 300 meters away, more than three times the length of a football field, the distance was not intimidating; I knew I was capable of swimming much farther than that.

What did intimidate me was standing there in my bathing trunks among the other contestants, a group of the strongest, most athletically-built campers who had amply demonstrated their exceptional skills all summer in the sports we played daily: baseball, football, track and field, volleyball. However, the only swimming we did was not competitive, but recreational. Once a day we all jumped into a roped-off section of the lake and horsed around. There weren't any lanes for swimming laps, just one large area for cooling off under the watchful eyes of the lifeguards.

What also intimidated me before the race was the same thing that embarrassed me during those daily swimming periods: showing my body. A decade of rehabilitation had given me movement, but did nothing to change my appearance. My left shoulder blade was displaced and my left shoulder was rounded and hunched forward. My left arm stuck out at an angle, the elbow elevated, very much in the crooked position women use to dangle a purse. Though both of my arms are the same length, the left appears shorter, since it is always bent, and my left arm is noticeably thinner, the biceps smaller, than the right.

Simply put, I felt humiliated to be seen without a shirt on. People stared at me. I was a curious sight. Polite onlookers quickly averted their eyes and said nothing. The impolite stared and said things I did not want to hear. There were questions from those whose curiosity got the better of them. "How did you get that way?" "Did you break your arm?" Then there were the taunts— "Jerk," "Shithead"—from exasperated team-mates when, once again, I failed to catch a ball. One of the characteristics of my Erb's Palsy is that my left arm does not rotate, so that when I attempt to catch a ball, instead of naturally forming a cup with both hands as others do, my left hand drops like a lid over my right and the ball usually bounces off the top of my left hand.

That is, if my left hand is under the ball. It could be anywhere. A peculiar concomitant of my nerve damage is a loss of "proprioception" in my left arm. Proprioception is the sense we have of where our body parts are and where the body is in general relative to its surroundings. Such information is handled on an unconscious level and transmitted to the brain from neural sensors all over the body; the brain then uses this information to move muscles and tendons appropriately. My problem is that some of the neural sensors in my left arm have been damaged or destroyed, so that they can't inform my brain where my arm is in the usual way. Instead, I've learned to use my eyes to provide this information to my brain. This alternative system works pretty well, but is relatively slow. It is as if most of my body operates on a high-speed broadband network, while my upper left quadrant calls in on a long-distance telephone line. In practice it means that if I don't think about it and don't look at it, I don't know where my left arm is or where I'm going to put it. That's why my jutting left elbow and forearm are often black and blue, because at least once a week I bang them on the side of a doorway as I pass through. Trying to scratch the back of my head with my left hand is a major undertaking.

There is another peculiar thing about my left arm: it has a life of its own. That is, because of the arm's damaged neural circuitry, because it is not properly hooked up to my brain, there is involuntary movement. The usual action is a gentle palsy, tremors, shaking. Sometimes there is a livelier twitching and my hand moves a few inches this way or that. The most bizarre movement is an unexpected, almost violent jerk of the entire arm, the sort of exaggerated motion you might make when tossing a frisbee. At a party I once flung a plate of canapes clear across the room! What do you say to someone you have just pelted with a fusillade of Swedish meatballs? I do not remember. I do not want to remember.

What I will remember always is the beginning of the race across the lake at camp. Not the jostling and shoving, the shame I felt about my flawed body among the well-proportioned physiques of my competitors, my hesitation amidst their eagerness. What I do recall—feel now as I write—is my dive into the water, the one element on this earth that hid my imperfections. There was no sense of transition from the sounds in the warm summer air, the bright sunlight, the green of the landscape into the relatively quiet cool and translucent blue of the water. The change was seamless. I was at home.

Staying in a shallow dive just beneath the surface as long as possible, I immediately set my kick in motion, scissoring stiff-legged in a short up-and-down that left almost no wake.

Breaking the surface with head cocked to the left, I sucked in air, quickly put my face down again and began my strokes, alternating three with each arm, slowly exhaling until I needed to breath again. I concentrated on this sequence, which I had practiced in rehabilitation thousands of times.

Around me there were frog-kicks and gyrating arms as the other swimmers crashed through the water. For them forward progress meant pitting their youthful energy in powerful bursts against the resistance of the water. It was a matter of strength. For me it was a matter of form, holding true to it consistently. I did not seek speed. In fact, I held back slightly, as I always did, reducing the pull of my right arm, the stronger of the two, in order to swim in a straight line and not drift to the left. When I did all of these things well I knew it. There was little sense of resistance. I did not push or pull against the water. It was as if I hardly touched the liquid I moved through. And all this was done in the grace of silence.

Well, let me get right to it. I won the race. And let me say that my emergence from the lake, a good ten meters ahead of the second-place finisher, was for me the least important event of that day. I will explain in time.

My immediate thought as I stood up in the shallow water and ran splashing onto the beach was not exultation, but haste to find a towel to cover myself. As soon as I did, and the water cleared from my eyes, I saw the crowd, virtually the entire membership of the camp, on the beach. There were no cheers. Silent, eyes wide, mouths agape, those campers and counselors stared at me in amazement.

You know, it was not until many years later that I first heard the term, "cognitive dissonance," which is the discomfort you feel in your mind when you see or hear something that contradicts what you believe to be true. There on that beach an entire crowd had just witnessed what none of them had imagined possible: that odd-looking, clumsy camper, the one who could not catch a ball, who could not keep up, who was always chosen last, had just won the day's most arduous athletic event. I stood there in front of them, wrapped from neck to knees in my towel, trying to hide from their stares. The towel pulsated, because underneath it my left arm was palsying.

We maintained this mutually uncomfortable face-off for what seemed to be an eternity, which ended when the other swimmers began emerging from the lake. There were cheers then. And finally my bunk counselor and a few friends moved toward me to offer reserved congratulations and expressions of their surprise. None of the other contestants said a word to me, though. Why they said nothing was made evident when the camp photographer tried to get the three top finishers together for a picture. The second- and third-place winners refused. One of them said, "I don't want anybody to know I lost out to someone who looks like him."

At the time I was more confused than humiliated. Used to losing, I was unprepared for victory. I was accustomed to rejection and complaints about my performance. But I had won the race! It was only later, that night on my cot in the bunk house, the lights out, just before falling asleep, that I began to put my thoughts and feelings into some perspective. And it was that perspective, though limited by my youth and inexperience, that became the basis of how I would deal with my disability throughout the remainder of my life.

First of all, it was evident to me that I had been ill-treated by my fellow campers. Their silence as I emerged the winner of the race arose from their surprise, but it was also mean, uncharitable. So was the refusal of the other racers to be photographed with me. It was not my inadequacy; it was theirs. All of my life I had looked at myself when criticized or taunted—and found myself wanting. After all, I really did not look like other boys. But I had won the race! I deserved my due. I was angry. And so began my inclination to listen more to my inner voice and less to what others said I was or wasn't. I now try to acknowledge my anger—and express it in healthy ways—when I am treated unfairly because of my handicap. As an adult I do not easily tolerate pity or ridicule or impatience or any sort of abuse when a failure to understand handicap is the cause of it. I am apt to climb upon a soapbox when the Americans With Disability Act is mentioned. Forgive me, but there is a chip on my misshapen shoulder.

The next thought I had there upon my camp cot may sound contradictory: it was really not that important that I had won the race. While winning or losing obviously was very important to others and determined their behavior towards me, I was not really excited by my victory. Long before that afternoon I had become aware that much in my world—say, in the schoolyard games we played, in how we were judged by our looks—was a competition and that in such a context I was doomed by my disability to be a "loser." In addition, try as I might, I never fully understood the importance of being "the best," "number one," "the champ." Why should being "first" make you happier than being "second" or for that matter "last"? Such competitive rankings seemed to me entirely separate from what was really important: that is, "excellence," "doing your best," "making the most of what you had." When I employed these last standards my disability was not a handicap, but a fact of life. And so what counted was that I had made it across the lake in good form, not the order of my crossing. My life has been led accordingly. I have not won other races, but I have known fulfillment. And my successes have been measured not in terms of where I stood in line, but rather how I have helped myself and others to realize their potential.

All this, of course, evolved from the thoughts of that twelve-year-old who lacked the sophistication an adult would bring to bear on dealing with disability. On the other hand, those of us who were disabled children were precocious in this regard: we were forced to confront the most serious aspects of our human frailty, even our mortality, long before our peers. I came to understand early on, for instance, that my rehabilitation sessions were sacrosanct and could not be postponed by my moods or evasions if I wanted to regain movement in my arm. Nor could pain or discomfort or inconvenience serve as excuses to avoid what had to be done if I were to expect change. I learned I could not hide in my room from other children to escape the shame I sometimes felt in their presence. I had to accept that there were limits to what rehabilitation could do for me, to accept that I would always be impaired and that there were certain things that I would never be able to do. I also had to understand that I possessed worth and that the road to the future in many areas of my life was unobstructed by disability.

So, there in the dark on my camp cot, reflecting on the day's events, I was very young, but not entirely naive. Disability had long made it imperative to honestly assess my innermost thoughts and feelings. Such introspection is a gift that the disabled are offered to help overcome their handicaps. Most of us accept it. When we do we can be the equal of all men and women, even more able than most, because of our experience in dealing with adversity.

Robert S. Kahan, Ph.D., 74, lives with his family in Johnson City, Tennessee, far in place and time from his native New York City. He is retired after a career as a university professor and administrator, as well as a communications specialist for media, business, government, and non-profit organizations here and abroad. He can be reached at robertkahan@comcast.net.

The First Star I See
W. Burns Taylor

Suddenly, he was there in the doorway—Jimmy, my brother—with the rifle in his hands. Raising it to his shoulder awkwardly, he cocked the bolt back hard, paused, then clacked it shut: ftaking aim, certain that it wasn't loaded.

"You wanna play cowboys?" he asked, pretending the gun he gripped was primed to fire. He took a step forward into the room toward me.

"No," I said. Not because I didn't want to play, but because my brother's voice sounded menacing, deceitful, like when he tricked me into doing something that scared me or that I got punished for later. Still, I stretched out my arms to be lifted out of my crib.

Jimmy drew a bead on the bridge of my nose and touching the trigger ever so faintly, like a child stroking a robin's egg, he wondered what would happen if the gun were really loaded.

If it shoots, he thought, Burns'll probably die and after that, they'll kill me. But it won't; it can't.

Then—for one moment, one flickering instant—something caught in his throat and his finger faltered. The magnitude of the event unfolding hypnotized him. He waited and listened in vain for a sign, a voice that would oppose him. Finally, braced for the clink of the hammer against an empty chamber, his finger followed through. But he knew as soon as the trigger glided into motion that the game was over.

"I've killed him! I've killed him!" he yelled. "My brother's dead."

Flinging the gun down, he raced outside across a narrow yard to the trailer where my father slept. Dad was working graveyard shifts at the Houston Shipyard and sleeping days.

"When I heard you scream and came to see," my sister told me years later, "you were slumped down in the baby bed crying bloody tears all over the place. It scared me to death, so I ran and hid under a bed in the other room with Bubba and Elaine."

Less than a mile away at Dupuis' Grocery, my mother was standing at the checkout counter when a neighbor boy came banging through the front door shrieking the incredible news at the top of his voice. She left the store on a dead run, forgetting she had gone for groceries in the car.

At the hospital, seventeen miles from home in Port Arthur, Texas, surgeons rushed me into the operating room for emergency treatment. My right eye ruptured and was removed immediately. Pellets from the .22 caliber rat shot had permanently severed the optic nerves leading from my brain. There was never any doubt in the doctors' minds that I would be totally blind from then on. And I was.

My new life began with a long, lean scream on that Saturday morning in 1944 when I was just three years old, and heaven blew up in my face. The world came looking for me out of the barrel of a gun, gave me its best shot, and I survived. Now, it was up to me, with the help of my family, to pick up the broken pieces of my world and make a new life as a blind person.

But the shadow of that single event fell across the life of each member of my family. It was, curiously enough, the source of our strength and unity, and at times, the fuel of our despair.

My own adjustment to blindness was made simpler because of my youth. Still, the impact was tremendous and far reaching. For about a year following the shooting, I was bothered by petit mal seizures. A typical attack began without warning in convulsions that tapered off into unconsciousness. One day I keeled over into a lighted space heater. Gradually, though, my seizures were controlled by a daily dose of Phenobarbital, and eventually, they disappeared altogether.

It was the emotional shock of being blinded in such a traumatic way that was the most devastating though. One particular nightmare terrified me night after night. I was floating down through the sky toward two old hags who danced around on the ground beneath me. As I drifted down within reach, they clutched me in their bony fingers and hurled me back up into the sky, cackling wildly.

Anger and hostility proved to be the most troublesome emotions for me to learn to handle. A ball of negative energy would well up inside of me and threaten to blow me apart if I didn't let it out. So I mutilated my toys and smashed rocks and bricks with a hammer for hours on end. I made soldiers out of modeling clay and chopped them to pieces, incessantly, with a knife on my mother's hard wood floors.

At times I was stricken by spells of profound loneliness and isolation. They came over me unexpectedly, like a trance, cutting me off from the rest of the world. Sometimes, even in the midst of boisterous play with other children, their voices would fade away and become muffled. And I imagined that I was marooned on the edge of a huge lake. All I could hear was wind in the trees, water lapping against the shore and far, far away, the buzz of talking and muted laughter. But not for me.

I felt stranded in an alien place, lost and blind, with nothing but the sound of my own words to comfort me. I was afraid to take a step for fear of falling over a rock and into the water.

And just then, at the very peak of my desperation, I'd hear a long, loud, reassuring yell from the other side of the lake. It would always be my sister's voice saying, "Hey you! Better get your butt back over here. It's your turn now. Cummon, I'll show you how."

Gwen was the one who told me about sunsets and rainbows. She'd raise my hand and pointing at the evening sky, we'd chant in unison, "Star light, star bright; the first star I see tonight..." She mystified me with her vivid description of colors and the other miracles of sight. She was my eyes, my vision, my teacher.

Gwen learned Braille so she could make me play school with her on Saturday mornings. Three grades ahead of me, she'd give me the material once, then test me over it, reading my answers from the back side of the Braille page.

She wrote Braille letters to me when I went away for the summer. Those thick letters came like coded missives from another world in our own secret language. No one else could read them.

And the games. We'd play hide-and-go-seek, but my ears were so sharp that I could just step to the door and tell whether or not she was in there by the fullness of the room. So she'd hold her breath so the sound of her breathing wouldn't reveal her hiding place. But when I found her anyway, she'd make me play with cotton in my ears.

She had her diabolical side, too. I soon learned, through Gwen, not to expect the world to give me any quarter because I was blind. She exploited my blindness whenever and however it was to her advantage to do so: openly cheating on me at Monopoly, sneaking the raisins that she hated out of her oatmeal and into my bowl when I wasn't paying attention.

She put me through a course in jungle warfare like a boot camp drill sergeant. One of her favorite tricks was to get me up in the air on the seesaw—her end down—and then jump off. I'd go into a breathtaking freefall like a sky diver and thud to the ground in a heap. Or she'd test my reaction time by springing out at me from hiding places or by throwing obstacles in my path when I chased her. I developed the agility of a tight rope walker. My adrenal glands were working overtime. But if anybody else taunted me or took advantage of my blindness, she rolled in like the armored divisions of the First Infantry, the shock troops, the Marines up the beaches.

My sister was my friend and my adversary, but I was deeply in love with my mother in my early years. The separation from her when I started school was unbearable. I carried pieces of paper with the scent of her perfume on them in my pocket. Whenever I got lonely for her, I'd take one out—unfold it, sniff it and she was there with me.

Most of the time she treated me with tenderness and patience. Then she'd turn right around and whelp my legs with a green stick off a Chinaberry tree. Like the time I dumped a two-pound box of oatmeal into the gas tank of my father's old stake-body truck. She'd send my sister out to pick the switch. So if I was on Gwen's good side, she'd bring back a swisher. But if I'd crossed her, she'd come dragging in a limb the size of her thumb.

Willie Mae was my only hope, then. She was the Black lady who worked in my mother's laundry business. She did most of the cooking and house cleaning, too. She'd chide my mother for whipping me so hard.

Willie Mae was my protector and my conscience. She would fly into a rage if someone carelessly left a bicycle or toys lying in the way for me to stumble over. And she agreed to warn me whenever she saw that I was headed for trouble.

"All right, boy," she'd say, "you fixin' to get in bad." And I'd back off just a notch.

As a child, my mother always had the highest expectations for me. On Saturday mornings, my sister and I had to help her in the laundry she operated next door to our home. She had the old ringer type washing machines that flattened the clothes like pancakes. I can still feel how those rollers nibbled at my fingertips as I fed the clothes through. Then Gwen and I would hang the clothes out to dry on four long lines that stretched forty feet across the back of the building.

My mother had high expectations for me in school, also. In my studies at the University of Texas, she was there for me. She would get up at five o'clock in the morning and read my Latin lesson to me one letter at a time. Then she went to her eight to five job. In the evenings, she would read a chapter of anthropology or some short stories I needed for the next day.

My mother gave me her best and she expected me to give her back my best. She always admonished me to hold my head up and get out there, that I could do as good a job as any one. She told me never to let any person make me feel inferior because I was blind.

In the early Fifties, my dad decided to go into business. He bought a Gulf filling station about eight blocks down the highway from our house. It was a full-service gas station: an attendant put in the gas, wiped the windshield and checked under the hood as soon as Customers pulled in.

On weekends, my dad let me help out at the station. I learned how to raise and lower cars on the grease rack. Willie Menzetti, his mechanic, taught me how to do hot and cold patches on inner tubes. In those days, a bell rang for every gallon of gas that went through the pump. So if a customer wanted five gallons, I simply counted the bells. If I listened closely, I could tell when the gasoline began rising up the neck of the tank and cut it off.

I was ten years old. My dad taught me how to do oil changes and how to clean windshields with the chamois. I'd run the chamois through the ringer on top of the bucket at the end of the gas pumps. Then I'd wipe the customers' windshields and send them on their way.

But my father, who had always been a steady drinker, graduated to the class of rock-bottom, textbook, alcoholic drunk: the dry heaves, the D.T.'s the Sunday morning shakes. He could drink with the best of them or the worst of them. Or if need be—which it often was—alone, in the cab of his rattly old red pickup, swilling salvation through the neck of a bottle of Hill and Hill, rot gut whiskey at a dollar and ninety-nine cents per. So he soon lost the filling station and took up drinking fulltime.

My father became a make-believe character who was always going to take me with him, who loved us dearly—my mother said and wanted, more than any thing else in the world, for me not to grow up to be just like him.

And Jimmy, my big brother, was even more fictional than that. Nine years older than I, he came in and out of my world like a bit player in a B movie. All I knew about him from the time of the shooting until I was in high school was what I heard from others. Immediately after blinding me, he became an introvert—morose, shying away from the rest of the family. He avoided me like the plague. I embarrassed him in front of his friends and reminded him of something he needed desperately to forget.

His life already tainted by guilt and low self esteem on the eve of adolescence, he grew to respect meanness and insensitivity in people. He took up with a pack of teenage toughs who drank and carried guns—guys who could pull a dog's ear off with a pair of pliers without flinching. He got into bloody fights at school and was finally expelled for setting off a firecracker in the classroom.

A few weeks later, he and some friends thumped a cherry bomb into a United States mailbox and blew cards and letters all over a downtown street in Austin, Texas where we lived. When the smoke cleared, the only thing that saved him from facing federal charges for willful destruction of government property was that he was still under age. To appease the authorities and cool things down at home, he was sent away to the country to live with Auntie and Uncle Weldon, the same uncle whose rifle had blown my eyes out five years earlier, my name sake.

There was a sense in which Jimmy and I could never be brothers. We were like the X and Y of some perverse equation for human destruction and failure. I was his Albatross; he was my brother Cain. And yet our lives were welded together in an inextricable bond that went far deeper than brotherhood. We never discussed our feelings about what happened between us until I was well into college.

Those were the characters who traveled with me on the first leg of my long journey through the darkness of fear and vengeance—each of us isolated from the others by guilt or hate or madness. Each of them felt responsible, to one degree or another, for the tragedy that was our lot: my mother, because she left a house full of children alone with no adult supervision; my father, because he was asleep and my sister, too, because she said my father had always made her feel responsible for not intervening somehow, even though she was only seven years old at the time of the shooting. And my brother, most of all, because he stepped into my life one day like a god and changed it forever.

And I, for my part, was driven by the pressure of being the object of their collective guilt. I felt compelled to over achieve, to prove to them and to the world that there was no reason to feel guilt or pity or shame for me because of my blindness.

That pressure resulted in my achieving a long series of firsts: first of three blind students to enter the Austin public school system, first blind person to teach at the University of Texas at El Paso and El Paso Community College, first blind person to own and operate his own publishing company.

Over the years I learned to ride a bicycle, water ski, snow ski, overhaul automobile engines and play numerous musical instruments. I earned two college degrees, made a movie, won $12,000 on a national game show and have published poems and articles from coast to coast.

All of those accomplishments were possible only because of the love and support from my family. Each of them prepared me in a different way to survive in a sighted world. My sister gave me the faith it took to make a wish upon an evening star I could not see. My father taught me to always be ready to welcome a new challenge. But it was my mother who imbued me with the courage to stand up strong in the face of overwhelming odds and say, "I can."

In the end it was my mother who kept the family together and tried to heal our wounds. That sense of unity so vital to the meaning of family had been shattered. It was to take years of suffering and sacrifice before we could get it back.

Burns Taylor is an employment assistance specialist and freelance writer living in El Paso, Texas, with his wife, Valora. His works have appeared in Publishers Weekly, *the* Braille Forum, *and elsewhere. He was a featured performer and contributing writer on "Beyond Blindness," a one-hour documentary produced for PBS television.*

My Eyes and I
Kathy Nimmer

INTRODUCTION

I am a thirty-five-year-old woman. I am also a writer, teacher, crafter, daughter, mentor, walker, learner, leader, follower, and creator. I am many things, all touched in a profound way by the deterioration of my vision over a period of sixteen years. My blindness has shaped my destiny, personality, and aspirations. Throughout this manuscript, I explore through prose and poetry the particular relationship fostered over years of adjustment between who I am and my disability. It is a relationship of both victory and defeat, but it is most distinctly our story, an unfinished and ever-changing exploration of the human spirit, hope, and discovery. Come with me now to learn about "my eyes and I."

Every life story is one of tragedy and triumph; mine is no different. "My Journey Out of the Dark" highlights the individual walk that has been mine to travel with the progressive loss of vision as one of my constant companions. The foundational beliefs emblazoned upon my heart through this journey are what propels me forward each day.

MY JOURNEY OUT OF THE DARK

When I was a little girl, I could see the world spread out in front of me. This was true on a literal and figurative level simultaneously. I had perfect vision, and I had an enormous imagination. That imagination converted doll houses and their little figurines into real worlds with complex stories involving vivid characters who interacted with realistic intricacy. And let's not forget my fictional world of competing gymnasts who flipped and twisted on our backyard Jungle Gym with the girl bearing my favorite name always winning the gold.

And somewhere, I knew God was watching over me, guiding this shy and introverted dreamer toward a future of ... what I didn't know, but He was there. My bedroom was pink, my brother was only as annoying as siblings are allowed to be without crossing that forbidden line into enmity, and my pet dogs completed the picture of joy.

Then, life beyond my imagination slipped in quietly and swiftly. My parents divorced, we moved to a new town, and my vision started deteriorating. I went from doctor to doctor with the constant message that I was making up the vision problems to get attention. God seemed to have gone silent, especially the day that my mom and step-father heard the news that I would never drive and might experience enough vision loss to classify me as blind one day.

At age eleven, the doll house figurines, minus the doll house itself which was too cumbersome to pack up, accompanied me to a school for the blind 150 miles away. There, I found a future which was much different than I'd ever counted on. New challenges, new teachers, long and scary hallways which twisted and turned in spooky ways, … it was overwhelming. But, my keen interest in learning and dreaming emerged once more, and I felt my feet find a place on which to stand again.

Age fourteen swept away any pretence of being sighted for the rest of my life as I learned braille, crossing that line between the seeing and what I feared would be the unseen. After all, how could God allow loss at the most critical time of growth and development in a young girl's life? Where had He gone anyway? I slipped into anorexia and depression, clawing for control in my spinning universe. Those little figurines of childhood could help me escape no longer, and I was lost.

With the prayers of a minister from my home church and with the belief others had in hope, I began seeing a flicker of light in the darkness. My desire became to succeed, to find excellence, to soar above expectations and fill the emptiness with achievement.

And so, I did just that. National champion gymnast, head cheerleader, speech team member, writer, pianist, organizer, valedictorian, all titles I added to my resume. I used these successes to propel me into college at a small Christian school nearer home. There, I lost travel vision and began using a cane. But, I found a career that seemed to fit as I trained to be an English teacher. See, the characters who inhabited my childhood worlds now were leaping forward, out of existing books that I could bring to life for my students and also out of my own imagination and onto paper which was finding publishing opportunities. I felt God's presence again and knew He hadn't been gone; I'd just been turned the wrong direction.

After grad school, I interviewed with a maverick principal who liked to be "first." I was his experiment; he would be the first principal in our region to hire a blind teacher. Bravo for me, for it got me in the door. Had I any way to know what was behind that door, I might have turned and run back to the rusting and discarded Jungle Gym back at my parents' house.

My first years of teaching were one continuous haunting nightmare. Students slipped quietly out of my classroom, teachers didn't speak to me, parents didn't support my decisions, and chaos reigned. In the bleakest moment, right after a student's thrown book bag shattered a frosted glass window between my room and a nearby office, I contemplated quitting and starting over in some other career. I would have done this, but I had no idea where to start and no clear leading from God to make a move.

I prayed, harder than I ever had done before, even in the darkest moments of loss and change in the past. And, finally, a wall that had kept me from the constant knowledge that God loved me how I was, where I was, and His hand was in everything in my life, … that wall shattered like the frosted window in my classroom. I finally knew I didn't have to imagine, succeed, or flounder anymore: Jesus was my living, loving Companion, and I only needed to trust.

Nothing magically became "okay." But, I did have a new direction, a new hope. Dear friends who ran a ministry for the blind were pillars during this time of rebuilding. They knew already what I was just learning, and I looked to them for guidance. Gradually, classroom problems declined, and my sense of worth grew. Issues from the past which had been silent mocking forces surfaced and then slid into the corners of my existence where the loving presence of my Redeemer shadowed their supposed importance.

Now, I am finishing my thirteenth year of teaching. I walk with a beautiful guide dog by my side and with an assurance that God is using me in this public high school as a testament of hope. I falter and fumble, but then I stand strong once more. And, as in those imaginary outdoor games where the gymnast with my favorite name always won, I cling to the favorite name in my life with the sense of certain and eternal victory: my Lord Jesus Christ.

A significant part of my identity as a blind woman involves my career as a teacher in a sighted public high school. This next piece, "Being a Blind High School English Teacher," reveals some of the practical and personal challenges of this vocation. It also illuminates the reason that the extraordinary effort is worth it for me.

BEING A BLIND HIGH SCHOOL ENGLISH TEACHER

If you came into the public high school where I teach, you would know who I am. It isn't because I am the best teacher in the building or because I have the first classroom inside the main entrance or because there is a huge poster (or dart board!) with my picture on it in the foyer! You would know who I am because I am the only one who has a guide dog, the only one who can't quite tell if her classroom lights are fully turned on or not, the only one who doesn't notice the plethora of orange and blue accents meant to foster school spirit and unity. I am a blind English teacher, and my career world is one that has evolved from years of perseverance and adjustment, but I am where I am supposed to be, doing what I am supposed to do, eagerly seeking the next challenge that I am supposed to face.

If you recall your high school days, you probably remember that no day is "typical!" Between fire drills and convocations and parent/teacher conferences, the most valued quality of a teacher is flexibility!!! However, underneath the constantly changing chaos, there is a structure of sorts.

I arrive in the building at 7:00 A.M., having relieved my guide dog and already checked my e-mail. Before the students enter my classroom at 7:30, I consult with my classroom aide. I prioritize for her the things I need her to do or to have student aides do during the day (making copies, entering grades, grading objective quizzes, helping monitor activities, …); there is rarely time to discuss these matters once classes begin.

In our corporation, teachers instruct five classes a day, enjoy one prep period, and fulfill one "duty" which can be anything from study hall to lunch supervision. I teach all five of my classes in a row from first through fifth period, so that my classroom aide can be present during my teaching hours (most paraprofessionals are part-time with a cap of twenty-nine hours a week). My "duty" comes sixth period; I write the school's newsletter. Prep is seventh hour.

My five classes are usually packed from start to finish with activities, the best way to offset any potential behavior problems. My aide takes attendance, so I can begin teaching right at the bell. The most comfortable activities for me are discussions, dramatic reenactments, student-centered projects, games, and literary explication. Most challenging for me is group work (hard to monitor and access) and artistic projects (difficult to supervise and assess).

My classroom is very bright, cheerful, and organized. It is fun for me to hear the surprise in students' voices when they see that the "blind teacher" has a cool room! I require that students maintain an orderly classroom. Knowing there is a place for everything and everyone decreases the chances of me tripping, losing track of where students are, or misplacing things.

Before my classroom aide leaves for the day, I check in with her on the progress of the tasks we discussed earlier. Once she is gone, I either have student aides read assignments to me, go on the computer to prepare handouts and tests, or read over my braille teaching notes.

A reality of teaching is that the day does not end when the students leave the building at 2:30. I usually have between one and three hours of grading or planning to complete each evening. All teachers wrestle with those obligations, but blind teachers have more hurdles. I scan student work page-by-page into my talking computer. I occasionally hire English majors from a nearby university to check assignments for punctuation and spelling errors since scanners are not accurate enough to assess this kind of data. And, since no teaching resources are ever in braille, I have to develop my own materials.

No other blind teachers work in my region. Therefore, my colleagues are all sighted people with a variety of perceptions of me and what I do. Our department is made up of sixteen teachers; the school employs over a hundred educators overall. Do I feel fully accepted and integrated? No. Do I feel a bond of collegial companionship with anyone? Yes. However, I am convinced that some teachers still carry negative impressions of me, formed during my difficult first years as I figured out how to be a good teacher who was also blind. The standard discomfort some people feel toward those who are disabled is evident. I will never be able to do enough to be "equal" in certain co-workers' eyes. However, I like to believe that those people are few in number. Generally, I feel that I am a part of what makes our school a good one.

And those early difficult years, referenced above, were quite monstrous! I had no mentor teachers in the blindness community, little sense of how to work with the classroom aide who was eventually hired, and only a generic vision of how I wanted my classroom to operate, with no clue of how to get it there! It was trial and error and error and error, but I did find my answers and love teaching now.

My job is easier because of speech software, a multi-media projector that connects to the computer, my braille writer, a Talking Book Player, a scanner, my classroom aide, and volunteer student aides. Nothing is super high tech, but everything mentioned above is necessary and important. It is a formula of technology and coordination that works for me.

The best part of my job is the connection with the students. I love "knowing" them, figuring out what makes them soar and avoiding what makes them shrivel, filling them with confidence and showing concern when their hearts are heavy, being a model of determination and yet a very human, fallible individual. I love the creativity, the innovation, and the variety of each day.

I hate the paperwork!!!! Forms, memos, homework, tests, letters, IEP's, evaluations, catalogues, writing contests, agendas: these are my enemies! I am never free from paperwork; I can only hope to stay on top of it. Blindness definitely makes it a bigger monster.

You must be in love with your subject matter to pursue the career of teaching in a sighted school. If you are not, you will risk defeat by all of the things that make it seem nearly impossible. In my experience, there are very few blind teachers working with sighted students in the high school setting. It can be a lonely and intimidating career; you have to be committed to converting obstacles to opportunities and be that much better at what you do in order to make it work. More than all of that, you must love teens and love the interaction with them. Develop first-rate organizational skills, and know that you are teaching something more than your subject matter: you are teaching success, one poem or story or essay or novel at a time.

A liability that boldness and pride can create in the life of a disabled person is the forcing of action without thought, sending a fallible soul to plow ahead with a kind of "blind" disregard for dangers that could have been eliminated completely with a simple request for help. But, even in those moments of purest terror and doubt, we become more aware of abilities at the same time we realize our limitations. "The Crossing" captures one such moment of discovery.

THE CROSSING

The wind whipped through the open field, plastering my light-weight jacket so tightly against me that I had an illusion of warmth, even though its thin fabric was not suited to the early spring gustiness. I shivered with fearful uncertainty. Which direction is correct? Where am I? My guide dog Raffles huddled next to me, disoriented by the windy gusts and my panic. What should we do?

I'd finished my day's work at the part-time job I had taken with a local company that produced braille and technology for the blind. On top of hectic days as an English teacher at a public high school, five-hours-a-week spent testing products for the blind was occasionally very tiring but more often reaffirming. It was empowering to know my extra work was helping the members of the blind community of which I am a part. But this late afternoon held neither exhaustion nor satisfaction, just terror.

The company was a short mile from my house; I had wanted to walk home sometime to get used to the route and to assert my independence. That morning, I'd slid a talking compass, helpful in confusing locations, into my purse. I was determined to complete the journey that very day. Though the weather had taken a turn for the worse, pride wouldn't allow me to change my plans. After work, I'd headed out on the unfamiliar route, believing that I'd be safely home in less than fifteen minutes.

But I had forgotten to figure in the power of the swirling wind. For blind people, wind can be the ultimate enemy, stripping away the ability to hear, amplifying the challenges of blindness. Raffles was a seasoned veteran, but with no familiarity of the path and with the wind wiping away potentially helpful sounds, I didn't even know what commands to give him.

The talking compass told me I was facing east; Raffles's refusal to move forward confirmed that I was at a curb. Ah, could this be the intersection about a quarter mile west of my neighborhood? But there was no light or stop sign at that intersection, and the corner was curved and indistinct, preventing me from knowing exactly which direction would be a straight crossing. I found myself literally at a standstill.

Zzhhoooommmm!!! The powerful roar of a semi passing in front of me made me step back and nearly trip over Raffles. Probably, the truck wasn't even close to hitting me, but it did remind me that I was not alone. However, this was not a comforting reminder since its presence represented danger to me, not security. The drivers who spun past at 40 MPH were unlikely to sense my panic, and they easily could intersect any sightless crossing I might attempt. I felt alienated in general and totally separated from my destination in particular. And yet, I had to cross that road!

Lowering my head and closing my eyes, I said a silent prayer. Keep me safe; be my shield. I pulled Raffles to the edge of the curb, leaned forward to listen for sounds from the roadway, and stepped down onto the street. "Forward, Raffles." My voice was caught up by the wind and tossed away, but Raffles sensed my intent anyway and pulled ahead with urgency. Forward in faith, I echoed silently.

As I took my first step out into the street, I was vividly aware of the gentle up-slope of the road's rough surface under my feet. I knew that I'd be able to sense the midpoint of the crossing when the upward slope shifted downward; I'd be halfway to safety at that point. My feet carried me forward with erratic, scuttling steps, desperately seeking that slight change in surface: something, anything that could give me hope.

Then, about four steps out into the roadway, it happened. An uncanny peace engulfed all of me, both body and mind. Mentally, I knew that another semi could very well be bearing down upon me. The wind was so brutal that I wouldn't probably ever hear the roaring engine. But, instead of carrying visions of a horrendous crash, I simply was no longer afraid. Oddly, I felt as if I were somehow surrounded and protected, separate from everything and yet, most definitely and most peculiarly, not alone. The wind seemed no longer like a menace. I was held intact as if wrapped by a soft, enveloping blanket that held me securely in an interior world of peace and comfort. It became a cushion, a barrier against the wind, the traffic, and all danger … always. My feet which had been so keyed in on sensing the crest of the road's surface seemed now to be moving across a steady bridge, each step a bold and certain stride, not a groping and over-sensitized shuffle. I was confident that we would reach the opposite curb safely.

And we did. Raffles and I found the sidewalk on the other side of the street, and the talking compass confirmed that we were on the right track. I lifted my face toward the sky, offering a prayer of thanksgiving.

The inexplicable serenity of the crossing time left as quickly as it had come. Several large vehicles whizzed past us, thrusting ragged shreds of additional wind into the turbulent mix, pushing at my back like a high tide to remind me that we had just passed through our own version of the Red Sea. My heart began pounding violently again. My left hand, grasping Raffles's harness handle, cramped spasmodically. The chill of the March air seeped into my body, and I began to tremble.

By the time Raffles and I walked up to the door of my house, I was weeping with pain and fear. The journey had taken us over twice as long as I'd expected, but we were safe; we were safe. Praise God that somehow, in the midst of the swirling, impenetrable, deafening darkness, we were still lovingly, amazingly safe.

As the closing segment of this reflective manuscript, this poem shows where I am now: adjusted to a life influenced by blindness but also aware of the bigger picture. "We Three" is a message of hope, a mantra of acceptance. I love my life; blindness is part of that life, so I embrace it and the unique identity it gives me.

WE THREE

You smile
And I am unaware
Until your voice finds life
And joy bubbles through your words.
I see.

You cry
And I am unaware
Until your breath trembles
With the pain of unresolved heartbreak.
I see.

You question
And I am unaware
Until your hesitation flickers
Through doubting and uncertain footsteps.
I see.

You fear
And I am unaware
Until a shiver of clammy terror
Courses through your fingertips.
I see.

You discover
And I am unaware
Until you grasp my lonely hand
And lead me to discover too.
I see.

Wandering, cloudy, dim,
Filtering in only the sparse remnants of light,
Aching with the strain to focus,
Failing miserably,
Crafting a barrier of solitude,
Isolating me from those beyond the opaque glass,
Undependable, deformed, dead.

But, somehow, someway, somewhere,
We became a team, a dynasty perhaps,
A three-tailed comet flashing across the sky,
Burning an eternal pathway of hope, success, life:
You, my eyes, and I.

Kathy Nimmer is an award-winning teacher and writer (Eli Lilly Teacher Creativity Fellowship, Ned E. Freeman Excellence in Writing Award). Author of High Rainbows, *a young adult novel, she teaches English and creative writing at William Harrison High School in Indiana.*

Spinal Journey
John R. Killacky

This journey began eleven years ago in Minneapolis.

April 22, I was dozing. Larry was reading beside me in bed. An electric current entered my feet and pulsed through my body. Convulsion-like spasms lasted about fifteen seconds. As I regained consciousness, Larry was pressing on my chest, calling my name.

A visit to the doctor followed. After several MRI scans, I asked if they had found something or if the scans were inconclusive. The technician answered, "Yes." Larry asked her, "Yes, you found something—or yes, the films were inconclusive?" She replied, "I really can't say."

We learned that an ependymona—a tumor—was inside my spinal cord. It was located at the left side of the second cervical vertebra. Surgery was set for May 16. The neurosurgeon predicted I would spend three to five days in the hospital and fully recover in a month. Larry asked the doctor to describe the worst-case scenario. "In the case of catastrophe," he said, "breathing, motor strength, and sensation, as well as bowel, bladder, and sexual function, could be paralyzed."

Larry wanted to know everything about the surgery and its ramifications. I, on the other hand, chose to remain innocent of the details. Nevertheless, I wrote a will, naming Larry as sole beneficiary, gave him power of attorney and guardianship, and documented my medical wishes.

When friends arrived to witness the documents, I realized this might be as close as we would ever come to a commitment ceremony. Certainly it was as close as we could get to legally protecting each other, our relationship, and our meager assets. On our celebration cake was written: "When there's a will, there's a way."

It was still dark out when we checked into the hospital. I was put under anesthesia at 7:30 a.m. Eight hours later Larry was allowed into the recovery room. No one had prepared him for what he saw. I was covered in blood and iodine; incoherent, screaming, and paralyzed. If this was not worst-case, it was close.

Through a hallucinogenic blur of drugs, I tried to comprehend and name what had happened. Spirit, heart, and mind imploded as morphine, fear, and pain colluded. I remember little of that first week except Larry's face, my only connection to reality.

I was paralyzed from the neck down, my mind and body totally separate. No thought could will back movement, stop the spastic jerking of my limbs, or unclench my claw like left hand. I had lost the sense of where my left leg, arm, and hips were. After a few days, a miniscule amount of muscular contraction in the right arm and leg returned; yet I could not feel pain or register temperature on that side. Bladder and bowel control had ceased. I could not sit up by myself.

Frozen in this body, I fantasized about somehow getting to the window, breaking the glass with my head, and slitting my throat. Dawn was the worst— with Larry asleep and the medical shifts changing, I stared back at the world, whimpered, and cried.

Physical therapists cajoled the misfiring circuitry of my nervous system to release its stranglehold on my body. Improvement was agonizingly slow. Asked to set short-term goals, I had only one: "To walk again." "Start with things that are achievable," the therapist gently corrected me. "Toes and fingers. The rest may follow."

One day a nurse wheeled me to the sink for me to wash my face and brush my teeth. The left side of my face and shoulders was flaccid - sagging and lifeless; my head and neck were swollen, and the right side of my face was grotesquely skewed. I recoiled in disgust.

Denial became quite an issue for me. When Christopher Reeve was interviewed on television, I remarked how sorry I felt for the actor because he was quadriplegic. One of my doctors looked surprised and asked, "What do you think your condition is?"

I suffered from Brown-Squad's syndrome. This, the doctor explained, was an improvement from the quadriplegia that briefly afflicted me immediately following surgery. I had now progressed to a condition termed "paretic" (weakness or partial paralysis in all limbs), and was expected to be eventually "hemiparesic" (weak on one half of the body), with the numbness of my right side lingering indefinitely.

Indefinitely. Cruel word. I craved a precise timetable for recovery and badgered my medical team with questions. Every time I heard "anywhere from six months to a year," I wanted to scream. I demanded to know when I could return to work. When no projections were forthcoming, it occurred to me how thoroughly my identity, my sense of self, depended on my professional persona.

I took drugs for spasticity, inflammation, blood thinning, nausea, bowel regulation, sleeping, mood swings, urinary infections, migraines, nutritional deficiencies, and pain relief. Often, when a new medicine was introduced, side effects kicked in, sometimes multiplying in combination. Emotionally and physically I ricocheted from one extreme to another until I became pharmaceutically stabilized.

In therapy I worked alongside patients dealing with strokes or brain and spinal injuries. Two boys down the hall: motorcycle crashes screwed cages into their skulls. The elegant woman across the way: flawless on top, but her legs were dead, another surgery gone wrong. My roommate lost toes to diabetes and had another stroke.

I resisted being in group situations—not wanting to identify with the others, feeling safer in my own isolation. Seeing people worse off made me feel less sorry for myself, until someone more mobile showed up. Injuries to patients in their twenties were "tragic," recovering patients in their forties were "heroic," and those in their seventies "unfortunate."

Gradually my fingers began to unravel, toes began to wiggle, and ever so slowly my body responded to the prodding of therapists and loved ones. One night as friends were leaving I surprised them by painstakingly raising my hand and faintly waving good-bye. The first time I stood upright and took steps assisted with a walker and a leg brace, Larry and I wept.

Two weeks into rehab, the steroids and anti-inflammatory drugs caused internal hemorrhaging. I awoke in the middle of the night, choking on blood. "Get Larry," I pleaded. "I want to say good-bye." The burden was too much. Reassured he would come, I fell into a sublime state of letting go. Some time thereafter he shook me back to consciousness, crying, "Don't die on me." I returned through his eyes, words, and breath.

Blood transfusions stabilized me. When I was again able to practice sitting and standing, moving my left hand and arm, therapists encouraged me to venture out on short trips. I felt I was not ready. Some of my reluctance stemmed from fear I would be unable to navigate in a wheelchair. Part of it, though, was pride. I did not want to be seen in this devastated state.

The psychologist repeatedly explained that rehabilitation and recovery were separate. I had to get over the idea I was going to walk out of the hospital and reenter life, as I had known it. The sooner I learned adaptive behavior, the better off I would be. The average stay was four weeks. I was beginning my third.

Over the next two weeks I went on trips with other patients, including to the museum I worked at, Walker Art Center. Colleagues greeted me with sympathetic smiles, alarmed expressions, and open-mouthed pity. When asking how I was, few really cared to know, most needed to be reassured.

Together with doctors and therapists, we set a goal to be home by my birthday, June 24. I was given an afternoon pass for a trial run. Crossing the threshold, I broke down in tears, thrilled to be there, but intimidated. I learned how to walk up six stairs so as to be able to get in the front door. Now somehow I had to climb eighteen stairs to get to the second-floor bedroom and bathroom.

Back at the hospital, I packed in as much practical training as I could. I extended my tolerance for sitting up in a chair. I could know dress and bathe myself unassisted. Finally, as a last rehearsal of sorts, Larry and I spent an overnight in a transitional 'apartment' on the medical floor replete with videos designed for couples dealing with spinal injuries.

On my homecoming, friends presented me with a birthday cake. I found it difficult to express how much their love and encouragement meant. I needed them more than ever. Whatever independence I learned at the hospital did not translate in the world. Each trip became a lesson in overcoming unforeseen obstacles. Harder to accept was how society dealt with me. I was routinely referred to in the third person and assumed to be totally helpless. Each encounter made me smaller. Debilitation fueled self-loathing.

Friends took me on walks and drove me to therapy. My mother and sisters came to assist. I was grateful, but at the same time hated constantly asking for help. The more generous people were, the more acutely I felt my codependence. I was a child again, not knowing how to ask for what I needed, petulant when I sensed abandonment.

Outpatient therapy allowed motor skills, coordination, balance activities, and strengthening exercises to be fine-tuned and expanded. I went from using a four-tip quad cane to a single-end cane with a padded grip. My left foot became stronger and I could tentatively walk without a brace.

Gradually I began to use the cane more than the wheelchair. I noticed people assumed I was more stable with the cane than in the chair, although quite the opposite was true. After a few weeks I returned the hospital-loaned wheelchair; convinced it was behind me.

I deluded myself about the ease of returning to my job full-time. Merely walking down the hall to a meeting was an effort. Unable to drive, I could not go off-site to plan upcoming events with community partners. Full days at work depleted me, nights in the theater had to be rationed, and social gatherings with friends were nonexistent.

During this time, I was recruited to be executive director of Yerba Buena Center for the Arts in San Francisco. I could not imagine running a large organization while still learning to walk. Larry and my doctor gently reminded me that the Bay Area might be a better place weather-wise for my newly disabled body. Minnesota winters did seem unmanageable.

I accepted the job in November, a mere six months after surgery. A light snow was falling as we left Minneapolis to begin life in California. There were unexpected gifts. My new responsibilities helped me to stop mourning my old self—there was too much to do and learn. My new community only knew I shook at times and used a cane. In San Francisco's eyes, I had always been disabled.

Life at home revolved around getting to work and fitting in rehab. Weekends were spent in total collapse recovering from the arduous workweek. Ongoing physical therapy and pharmaceuticals combated lost kinesis, encouraging hope. On my right side extreme neuropathy persisted, with no ability to perceive sensation and temperature; on my left side I continued to experience spasticity, and an inability to sense location and touch. My bifurcated body was not aligned, torqueing with every step.

Needing to connect with others like me, I attended a disability arts conference. Blind and deaf people sat beside each other, worlds apart, waiting their turn to voice injustices. Actors railed against being brought on location to teach 'real' actors to mimic their actions. Artists who use wheelchairs wondered if they could only play their disability. As I joined others with stunted torsos, spastic limbs, and disconnected spinal cords, I was reassured I was not merely my disability.

I studied long-term survivors to see how their frames had adapted to changing circumstances, often by becoming increasingly bent. My doctors had said that could happen to me, but here was the real manifestation. I was frightened to hear of overtaxed compensating muscles waning in exhaustion after decades of unrelenting service.

My questions nagged at random moments: What to do with my anger? How to live with the ever-present pain? Will I ever stop wanting total recovery? How not give up hope? The people around me urged one another to celebrate the duality of the body and spirit, as well as the holiness of the breath, even on a ventilator. Everyone seemed so highly functioning and well adjusted; I did not feel comfortable asking about despair and desperation.

At this gathering, I was surprised to find internalized oppression subtly separating the quads from the paras, those with power chairs from those with manual chairs, even walkers from canes. Early-onset or congenital disabilities seemed more legitimate than degenerative conditions. Race, class, gender, and sexual orientation divided us. One quadriplegic comic derisively parodied Siegfried and Roy and the audience roared. My queer self was enraged at the homophobia and my walking self felt like a pretender as I left the conference.

Progress slowed and changes were infinitesimal, primarily measured in retrospect. Doctors told me function would probably return up to two years and then plateau. Not true I discovered through physical therapy, swimming, water running, Feldenkrais, chiropractic, and massage modalities. Five years post-mortem, my left hamstring began firing.

I read the body replaces its cells every seven years, so I then focused on the import of the seventh anniversary of my surgery. However, no miracles here. Time provided neither solace nor reconciliation. Though strength and range of motion improved, I did not have a balanced gait, which still necessitated using a cane.

Navigating deadened limbs and twisted trunk, pain remained constant. After a day's activities, I had no comfort left to give. Living through chemistry, libido was gone. Through an ongoing veil of chronic pain and depression, I longed for remembered sensations. However, sadness, anger, frustration, and tears remained private. During the day I was an arts warrior, public servant, and heroic crip.

One Christmas, I asked Larry what he wanted for a present. "A wheelchair, so we can do more things together," he replied. I worked so hard learning to walk; I viewed using a wheelchair as defeat.

He explained with a chair we could shop together, browse bookstores, and take the dog on extended walks. He wanted me to do it for him as much as for myself. He argued by not exerting so much, I might in fact extend my walking since neuropathy and weariness so limits my mobility.

My doctors and physical therapy team agreed. However, the insurance company did not. As a "community ambulator," coverage was denied. Wheelchairs were only provided for patients completely bedridden. It seemed oxymoronic. Luckily we were able to manage the finances and a few weeks later a black Quickie Rigid arrived with its wheels cambered like a racing chair.

Propelling the chair proved harder than I imagined; my fifty-year-old body had never engaged those particular muscles before and my condition made for an interesting challenge to exert equal force with both arms. However, within months I was building up endurance, time, and mileage as husband, dog, and I went out together.

I was embarrassed to be seen in the wheelchair. People asked if my health was worse. I found it impossible to tell them the chair actually improved my strength and vitality. And years later, I still only accept the chair as a recreational vehicle, never bringing it into work. Ego is a fragile and curious thing.

People get confused when they see me move in and out of my chariot. At the State Fair, I rolled up to the Tilt-A-Whirl and stood up to join the line. The ticket taker asked Larry, "Can he get on this ride?" "You better ask him," he replied. Being ignored in my chair infuriates me, but that day I just tossed it off and climbed on the ride, laughing as we zoomed around in circles.

I did hit another bump on my recovery road; blowing out my shoulder. Pain there and in my legs was such that I did not sleep and had a hard time concentrating. As anyone experiencing chronic pain can attest, exhaustion can be a physical and emotional state. After consultation, I added another drug to my maintenance plan and layered in new therapies, including acupuncture. With each knew modality of treatment however, I must interrupt my expectations—improvements are not cures.

My chair mileage is scaled back for now as I focus on micro calibrating muscle groups with more modest specificity. I do not know if I will work my mileage back up. Swimming, yoga, and meditation are current rehab priorities.

Four years ago I became the program officer for Arts and Culture at The San Francisco Foundation. In addition to my arts portfolio, I became a member of the Disability Funders' Network. In my new position I can advocate for changing the funding paradigm away from a medicalized perspective to one that builds upon opportunities for more fully integrated and richer lives for all of us.

Eleven years now into my spinal journey, what I hoped to be temporary must be accepted as permanent, although I continue to mourn the physicality I once embodied and dream of running unencumbered through the world. As I construct the days ahead, I still long for the life before. However, I try to intercept suffering, abide in discomfort, and forgive the trauma as I pray for clear seeing, acceptance without judgment.

Through these years, I learned about grace through the unwavering support of my husband, friends, colleagues, family, and new clan of crips who assisted with the emotional and functional challenges of living with physical disability. Not just their empathy, but all of them caring enough to ask how they could help and generous enough to really mean it. To them I am grateful.

John R. Killacky is the program officer for Arts and Culture at The San Francisco Foundation, as well as a video artist and writer. He co-edited the Lambda Award winning anthology Queer Crips: Disabled Gay Men and Their Stories.

Dependency
Stella Ward Whitlock

Recently, I was born again. Not in the sense of "born-again" Christian, but of starting life anew. At sixty-nine, after life-threatening back surgery, I found myself like an infant, dependent on others for my most basic needs: learning how to turn over, sit up, stand, walk, dress myself.

Thanks to the recall of Vioxx, the pain in my back from arthritis and degenerated discs had grown constant and unbearable. I could no longer walk normally or climb steps, and at night I woke my husband, Whit, by screaming in my sleep every time I turned in bed.

Soon I found myself at the office of my internist, who ordered X-rays, which indicated severe spinal stenosis, then an MRI, which showed compressed nerves and degenerative spondylolisthesis.

"Spondy what?" I asked.

"Spon-dy-lo-lis-the-sis," he repeated. "A condition in which vertebrae are so fractured that they slip and press on nerves." He walked to the small desk in the corner, turned his back to me, and made some unintelligible medical notes into a small tape recorder; I was patient #1799. He faced me again. "The nerve damage could be permanent if you go on like you are. I think surgery is . . ."

"No surgery!" I interrupted. "Aren't there other options?"

He examined the chart of medications in my thick file, laid it back on the table, and sighed. "Ordinarily, I could prescribe stronger, narcotic painkillers, but you've already gone through them. And you've tried all the stretching exercises and yoga." He paused and shuffled through my records again. "All I can do is refer you to a spine clinic specializing in noninvasive pain control."

This wasn't looking good. On the way home, I found myself practicing the word, chanting it like a mantra—spon-dy-lo-lis-the-sis, spon-dy-lo-lis-the-sis, spon-dy-lo-lis-the-sis.

•

Whit drove me to the spine clinic. The pain specialst took one look at my MRI and said, "I can't help you. You need a surgeon." She whipped around like a soldier and left the room.

Whit and I sat on matching plastic chairs, our fingers intertwined.

When the doctor returned, she told us that she had arranged an appointment for me with Dr. Paul Suh, a spinal surgeon, early the next morning.

That night I dreamed of being ten years old again, running in my red shorts and halter top through the field beside my house in Florida, twirling around and around in circles until I became so dizzy that I dropped to the ground, then buried my face in the cool grass until my spinning head and pounding heart slowed.

The next morning, Whit and I waited in silence in Dr. Suh's office. A slightly built Asian man with kind eyes and thick black hair, Dr. Suh walked quickly into the room, his movements abrupt, business-like. When he studied my MRI and medical records, he shook his head. "With any other patient, I'd recommend surgery," he began, "but with your health problem—heart arrhythmia, asthma, hypertension . . ."

My pulse was racing as if I'd run a marathon. "I don't want surgery!"

Dr. Suh made a "tisking" noise, as if I were a recalcitrant child. "I must tell you," he said, "surgery could cause a fatal heart attack, stroke, breathing crisis, or bleed-out."

He looked up from my records, cleared his throat, but didn't speak.

The room felt cold. I sat on my hands and tried to balance on the hard examining table. I thought of my grandchildren: four-year-old Whit, marching off to pre-school, backpack stuffed with the blue blanket I'd crocheted for him, his favorite Teletubby, and Green Eggs and Ham; Michelle, three, chasing bubbles, catching falling leaves; Andrew, six, killing dinosaurs or doing backflips on his trampoline. I felt vulnerable in that scanty blue cotton gown.

"Any other options?" I asked. "Acupuncture? Injections? Artificial discs?"

"Your vertebrae are too far gone for any other procedures."

Perhaps it was the hint of sympathy in his voice that made my eyes wet with self-pity.

With effort to control my voice, I clutched the untied ends of my gown and asked, "What would the surgery entail?"

"I'd have to remove crumbling bone, free compressed nerves, insert rods and screws, and pack the area with bone from your hip." He paused, tapped his pencil against a manila folder, and continued. "It wouldn't be simple. You'd be in surgery for about six hours."

"Sounds awful." I paused, then asked, "If I don't?"

"Your spine will continue to crumble, pain will escalate, and your legs will be completely paralyzed. Within six months you'll be completely confined to a wheelchair."

Dr. Suh waited patiently, his compassionate eyes watching my face change in the wake of his prognosis. Surgery terrified me, but the thought of endless pain and paralysis was worse. Something in me shifted as the words of Psalm 23 entered my mind: "Even though I walk through the valley of the shadow of death, I will fear no evil for you are with me."

I got brave. "Okay, let's go for it."

"It'll take at least a month to prepare you," Dr. Suh said. "To lessen the risk, we have to build you up. No choice. You need to start taking calcium and iron, stop taking prednisone and Coumadin, donate two pints of blood to use during surgery, and be thoroughly evaluated by a cardiologist associated with the hospital."

So began the saga of surgery prep: appointments with the cardiologist, the anesthesiologist, the assisting surgeon (who re-emphasized the dangers), the blood bank (for autologous donations of my O-negative blood), the BioTech company (for fitting the full-body brace I would wear for six months), then final clearance by my family physician and original cardiologist. Exhausting!

The morning of surgery, our daughter Elizabeth and our two sons, Linus and David, met Whit and me at the hospital. *They must think I'm not going to make it.* I wanted to walk out, but the thought of the prayers of my family and friends and the promise of God's presence comforted me.

Elizabeth went with Whit and me into the small room where a nurse told me to remove my clothes and slip into the usual open-backed hospital gown, this one white with a blue-flowered print. The slipper-socks were too small, so Elizabeth went to the nurses' station and traded them for a larger pair.

Then nurses noticed my wedding and engagement rings. "You'll have to remove those."

"I tried but I couldn't," I told them.

"You could lose your finger."

I tried again, pulling against my stubborn flesh.

"We'll have to cut them off." One nurse moved toward a steel cart.

I was almost in tears. I'd worn those rings for over forty-six years. A surgeon, overhearing the conversation, came to my bedside and took charge. He lubricated my finger, wrapped it tightly in strong flat tape, wound the tape around my finger, and pulled on my rings until they finally slipped off.

●

I opened my eyes—first darkness, then a long corridor of hazy light, everything out of focus, disconnected. Faces floated above me, concerned but benevolent. No bodies, no room, no context, just those beautiful faces. They smiled. I smiled back—or so they tell me—before disappearing into the abyss that would engulf me for the next week. I wasn't sure if I was dead or alive, but I was at peace.

Later, Whit told me that he and our children had been standing in the hall when I was wheeled past them from recovery to ICU. "You spoke to us, even called our names." He lifted my ringless hand and kissed it.

Only bits and pieces of the next few days remain. That whole first week after surgery, my world was foggy. I could hardly move. I remember mustering barely enough strength to extend my arms, hitting the bedrails, and thinking I had somehow been transferred to a crib. I was uncomfortable but couldn't even move my legs, much less turn over. Large hands appeared, rolled me onto my right side, then later my left, before leaving me alone.

Another memory is of half-waking during the night when nurses took vital signs. The sight of Whit on the nearby lounge chair reassured me. Although the lights were dim, I could see his chest rising and falling with every breath. I could feel the prayers of family and friends surrounding me.

I remember two women—nurses, I thought—who lifted me out of bed. They wrapped my hard, heavy brace around my body. Then they nudged me to the side of the bed, lowered the rails, sat me up, and helped me stand. To my amazement, I did stand, though for only a few seconds before collapsing. They caught me in their strong arms, praised my effort, and tucked me back into bed.

Still another time, a large African-American nurse in dreadlocks loomed above my bed. As he ran his gloved hands over my body, I slowly woke up. It was dark and his silhouette was outlined by fluorescent light from the hall. My mind was sleep-fogged.   Once he saw my eyes open, he apologized. "Sorry to wake you. Just giving you a bath." With that, I relaxed and enjoyed the comfort of the warm water, the silkiness of the baby powder, the gentleness with which he turned me onto my side, replaced my brace, and pulled the blankets over me. I was almost asleep again when he closed the door.

●

After that first blurry week, my mind—and eyes—began to focus. I remember Dr. Suh coming into the room. "Well, I'm till here," I said. "I didn't bleed to death, stop breathing, have a heart attack or stroke."

He looked me in the eyes. "You're not out of danger yet." He turned to his clipboard, made a few notes, patted my arm, and left.

I sank back against my pillow. Outside my window, trees whipped back and forth. Light faded as the sun dropped behind the trees. I closed my eyes but reopened them immediately, not wanting to miss anything. The day was ending, and I was still here—against unfavorable odds. I knew I was going to make it. I had indeed walked "through the valley of the shadow of death" and God was still with me.

●

One day, the two women—physical therapists, I now knew—came, propped me up in a wheelchair, and rolled me down a long hall. We entered an enormous room filled with people—some lying on tables, moaning, raising their hands and legs; others working out on machines. Two were riding stationary bicycles, others walking on treadmills or between parallel bars. A few, like me, were in wheelchairs. The therapists stood me up and supported me between them. My knees buckled, but the women held me tight.

As the days passed, my strength increased, and I got better at standing. The therapists began to time how long I could stand before my legs gave way. I struggled to stay upright, felt my knees trembling, and swayed until they caught me and eased me back into the wheelchair. One time I stood for thirty-nine seconds, and everyone in the room cheered. I felt proud.

When I finally could stand erect for a full minute, the therapists began teaching me to walk again. People supported me on each side while I held on to a walker. At first I could only shuffle my feet along the floor one or two inches at a time. Gradually I grew stronger and began to lift my feet, taking actual steps—three, five, nine, twenty. But still I leaned heavily on the walker and couldn't move forward without help. It was scary—no wonder toddlers cling so tightly to furniture and fingers. With every shaky step, I feared falling.

Days and nights ran together. I would lie alone in my bed, listening to hushed voices in the halls, footsteps hurrying back and forth, carts carrying medications and meals, announcements blaring over the intercom: "Ms. Shelly, you're needed in Room 705" or "Room 714 needs assistance."

I thought, what have I done to myself? Will I ever get out of the hospital? Ever walk again? Lead a normal life? At times I felt that my decision to have back surgery was a huge mistake, that I should somehow have managed to live with the pain, dosing myself with heavy-duty painkillers that dulled my mind as they dulled my pain, being wheeled wherever I went. Even in bed, I had to wear this hard-shell, full-body brace—uncomfortable, unflattering. Perhaps it would have been better had I not awakened after surgery. I didn't want to spend the rest of my life being cared for like a baby.

Visits from family and friends were the highlights of my days. Despite the eighty-mile drive from home to hospital, Whit came nearly every day of the month that I was there. He always brought me clean clothes, flowers, and magazines or newspapers. My children made frequent visits, too. Martha gave me a container of homemade party mix, Linus loaned me books on tape, David brought his portable DVD player with homemovies of my grandchildren, Elizabeth baked cookies and brought them with colorful pictures painted by my four-year-old grandson.

Several friends also made the long drive to cheer me, bringing treats of candy, fruit, and favorite foods like turkey and dressing. Many who couldn't come in person sent flowers and cards and phoned me. These connections with the outside world breathed life into my stale hospital room.

All the outpourings of support kept me going, helped me to get past the frustration and humiliation of total dependency—of being unable to walk, dress, bathe, even go to the bathroom by myself. Of having to push the call button and hear that embarrassing public announcement, "Leon, you're needed in Room 714," which usually meant that he had to get me out of bed, wheel me into the bathroom, position me on the raised commode, wait until I finished, and then put me back to bed.

I could lie in bed and see the bathroom just yards away, but it might as well have been a foreign country. One day, right after I'd learned to transfer from bed to wheelchair, I decided not to ring for help. I wheeled myself into the bathroom and pulled up by the sturdy grab-bar onto the raised seat of the toilet. There I sat triumphantly until I realized that I could not reach around that heavy brace to wipe my own bottom! So, I had to ring for the aide, who scolded me as if I were a disobedient child.

"Ms. W, don't you ever do that again! What if you'd fallen?" He assisted me into my wheelchair, put me to bed, and parked my chair across the room, out of my reach. "Now, you call us when you need assistance!"

●

Five months have passed since my surgery, and I can now walk with a cane. It's good being back in my own home, sleeping in my own bed, and returning to my work as a college writing instructor. I have only one more month to wear this hard-shell brace that immobilizes me from tailbone to collarbone, preventing me from twisting or bending and from doing many of the little things people take for granted. I'm thankful for an assortment of ADLs (Aids for Daily Living)—a flexible-plastic sock board, elastic shoelaces, a long-handled shoe horn, a grabber, a long-handled bath sponge, and personal hygiene tongs.

If I drop a pencil, I can't pick it up without my grabber. If something weighs over five pounds, I can't lift it. If a door is heavy, I can't open it. If the distance is more than fifty yards, I can't walk it. I can't climb stairs yet or even take a shower by myself. I still discover new things I can't do, simple things that were once automatic. I can't change sheets, reach bottom shelves of the refrigerator, unload the dishwasher, transfer wet laundry to the dryer, or pour from a full gallon of milk. Shaving my legs and cutting my toenails are impossible.

Sometimes, propped up in Whit's lounge chair, exhausted by life, I struggle with self-pity. But how can I complain when many people live with far more limitations? During surgery, I might have had a stroke and lost my ability to think, talk, or walk—or been paralyzed, bled to death, suffered a fatal asthma attack or heart failure. So I remind myself that my limitations are small and temporary.

Looking back at the person I was, I realize that I've been given a whole new life. My days are no longer dominated by agonizing pain. Moreover, my priorities have changed. I better appreciate my husband's devotion, his sacrifices, his willingness to perform the most menial tasks for me. I cherish each moment with my children. I enjoy playing games with my grandchildren, reading to them, listening to their stories, watching them play. I have more empathy for those with disabilities, whether physical, mental, or emotional.

Looking ahead, I wonder what the future holds. Will I need more surgery? Will I spend the rest of my days surrounded by those I love? Will I live to ninety-nine, like my mother, confined to a wheelchair in a nursing home and dependent on others again?

No matter. Whatever comes, I'm ready, grateful for my second chance. Life is good. "Surely goodness and love will follow me all the days of my life . . ."

Stella Ward Whitlock is a writer, the wife of a Presbyterian minister, the mother of four adult children, and the grandmother of seven. She has taught English for forty-five years at the elementary, secondary, and college levels. Currently, she teaches writing part-time at Methodist University in Fayetteville, North Carolina.

Two-Thirds of a Trilogy
Elizabeth Folwell

In spring 2003 I taught creative writing at a federal prison near Saranac Lake, New York. The program was one of three funded by the National Endowment for the Arts and the Department of Justice, with ten writers from different disciplines—poetry, fiction, journalism, screenwriting—doing month-long seminars. Our students were in the medium-security facility for a variety of crimes, but oddly, in all our classes, exactly what they were in for never was discussed. Instead we talked about isolation, enforced dependency, limited access to what gives us information, the structure imposed on our lives by others and how we tend to be defined by the simplest terms, stripped down to one word that sets us apart and declares our worth. For them, "felon"; for me, "blind."

As a blind person I had plenty to say about those constraints. Being unable to read a person's expression, losing the sheer joy of holding a book and understanding the words on the page, waiting for a ride to somewhere outside my limited confines all resonated with the men. While I could come and go through the metal detectors, sally ports and numerous gates, much of what I can do is determined by somebody else.

To our first class I navigated down the corridors with an escort, my white cane sweeping the parameters of our pathway. I put it in the chalk tray as students were filing in. I set down a few rules (no profanity unless it was an absolute necessity to the story) and a few suggestions, such as don't raise your hand to join the conversation, just speak. It dawned on the dozen or so men that they were beyond my comprehension except as movement and shape. From the back of the room came "What do we look like to you?"

I thought for a second, trying to be diplomatic. "Clouds."

From another side of the room, "White clouds or black clouds?"

At that we were all laughing. "Let's leave it at clouds. When was the last time anyone thought of you as something floating freely in space? You have no feet, no features, to me, and there you are. Unattached to anything, existing in air."

The title of the course was "Elements of the Essay," and the idea was to draw a bigger picture based on our experiences. Fair enough. I brought in personal narratives about the craft of writing from Barbara Kingsolver (she did not fly with my guys), Lawrence Block, Stephen King, Anne LaMotte, Terry McMillan, Richard Seltzer (they felt he was a show-off). It was a strange mix of authors, popular and obscure, but they all had things to say about the process of setting words on paper. E. B. White won the day, with a piece from the 1940s about calling oneself a writer and how a long prison sentence could be the impetus for great work. We talked about anything, from the relationship of music to architecture to crazy theories about the World Bank and the IRS, which circulated through the prison like the flu that spring.

In the first session I outlined our topics: greed, fear and hope. I also said no papers would be turned in, all works would be read aloud if the writer felt like sharing, and that we all would critique the pieces. What came from the students ranged from identifying a best friend's body after a shooting to burying an infant son to "my first TV set" to a dessert frenzy that bordered on pornography, so passionate was the author's desire to consume any cookie, cake, ice cream sandwich or candy within reach. I said I would also do the assignments, both to see how difficult it would be to summarize these themes in a page or two and to understand why I thought such topics were worthwhile.

The goal of my session and the entire yearlong program was not social rehab but to help the good writers in the twelve-hundred-bed facility really concentrate on developing their skills. Following are my pieces from the essay course, unpolished and thus far unpublished. I do not know what my students have done with their work, but I suspect that some pieces have grown into longer narratives, a few became spoken word performances and that at least one was sent to a mother in faraway North Carolina.

FEAR

"What is this stuff?" I ask. A young woman has slid a needle into the big vein where my elbow bends, and a orange fluid is flowing from a plastic bag in her hand.

"It lights up the tumors." She seems awfully upbeat, considering this news. I am stunned. I didn't know tumors were the unknown in the equation. But the other tests, from multiple MRIs to CT scans to spinal punctures have offered up no explanations for my problem. Even after months of hunting we still have no diagnosis, and it's very hard to embrace a disease that has no name, much less muster the resolve to deal with it, pragmatically and emotionally.

I take my place in the small, cold waiting room among other people who are dressed in tissue-thin cotton gowns and wrapped in blankets. We look like shipwreck victims, which is an accurate picture of our situations. Our ailments had tossed us, puzzled and powerless, up on some alien shore. We are all waiting our turn for rescue, today in some nuclear medical device, some modern electronic tool that would shed light on the mystery of our body failings. I am the youngest person in the room by twenty years.

I lost sight in one eye suddenly, painlessly, inexplicably. The best eye doctors in the Northeast were baffled. My optic nerve had pushed out part of my retina, distorting what I could see, and then all filled in with darkness. The transformation took five days from 20-20 vision to murk. I should have been scared, but I was in awe of the process. Now you see, now you don't.

My job that day (and there were many days of submitting to giant machines) was to lie motionless for four hours while a huge donut-shaped camera scanned my entire body. The thing was in a room like an ordinary kitchen, with a long formica counter and cabinets, and the platform under the camera was comfortable enough. I looked up at the ceiling—not that I had a choice—and was surprised by all the dead flies stuck in the fluorescent light fixture.

The time crawled. My mind wandered. After more than an hour I realized there was a little video monitor on top of the rotating apparatus, and I could see a tiny ghost picture of my insides. I saw finger bones, thought about wiggling my thumb, but stopped myself. I didn't want to get busted. I didn't want to start over.

Lying still, brain idling, for a while I felt plain old dread, the kind of fear of meeting something head on that you can't avoid. I dreaded the answer—yes, a tumor; no, we still don't know. For a time I worried, what comes next? I fretted about little inconsequential things like do we need to buy eggs after we leave here? Is there enough dog food for the week?

Fear, the real deal, is all about loss. Dread, worry, panic and terror are parts of the spectrum. Loss of life, love, freedom, power, now, those are things or events to fear. Can you face down these demons? Sometimes, with humble honesty. More often, there's a lie at the center of our defiance., something we do to shelter other people or avoid what we know is the clear, hard diamond of truth. A friend once explained the three stages of man as hubris, humiliation and humility. Most of us are stuck in the first or second step. Humility is saintly territory most of the time; for ordinary mortals it's the cartoon jack-in-the-box, an unexpected punch in the face, an event that only later is seen to be a gift or a viable way of life.

After losing the sight in my other eye, just as quickly, I am no closer to understanding what happened to both optic nerves. I am closer to knowing about heartbreaking fear, life-changing terror and the dread of knowing there is no simple repair for my situation.

Acknowledging these has given me an odd sense of freedom. Living with a profound loss has made me look hard, and inward, to respect the gift of life and the sure release of death. Dying is another matter. We don't get to choose how that happens. But I have learned how a complicated organism can quit in miniature accidents, and comprehend how an entire life can simply stop. It leaves me cold around the heart, but not scared. It leaves me humble.

GREED

All roads are good. I read that someplace, or maybe it was the title of a museum exhibit. Or maybe it was something someone said when we pointed the car into red rock country on a day of piercing sunlight and color so harsh it was painful.

There were trails everywhere from the parking lot, where tour buses idled as the crowds wandered and stumbled up to the rock formations. I couldn't get away from them fast enough; I did not want to share this day of aching brightness in a alien territory. All around were canyons, walls, towers, bridges, hills and hollows of red, orange, yellow and rust. The stone was powdery, like if you scuffed your feet you could grind the surface into spices, things like cayenne, paprika and turmeric.

From the spider web of pathways through treeless wilderness, we threaded among complex, austere forms. Here at Arches National Park was naked geology, undisguised by dirt or brush, unbroken by green. Bold, hard-edged shapes piled on top each other, and elsewhere, strange softness was made from stone itself.

Atop a sidewalk-smooth trail, which dropped hundreds of feet away on each border, I could see only more spice rock bridges to nowhere, only blue sky on and on. The horizon—what horizon?—was all around me, full circle, not a wall or a line or the edge of other buildings. The sensation was being inside a huge painted bowl. I could turn and turn, always looking at something otherworldly.

There were no houses in my field of view, not a thin strip of black asphalt, not a sapling, not even the contrail of a plane in the sky. The view was endless, and it was only right to want the day itself to never end. I wanted that more than anything, endless day, endless view, endless beauty.

I did not want to own a single thing I could see. I had no desire to even take a picture, or pick up a loose pebble. What I wanted was nothing but more, pure more, in an immediate, unadulterated hunger. Time had to stop for this greed to be satisfied, but we moved on.

Time did stop, I know now, because I can call up the memory of the landscape and my response to it. That longing is as real now, seven years out, as it was the moment I understood the sweep of untouched remoteness. I was nothing at all in this terrain, not even a breeze or a scudding cumulus vapor. Now that my eyes fail to comprehend color, depth and the panorama of mountains or even a city street, I call up this scene to comfort and console. Beauty is, and was, and can still be in my mind alone.

HOPE

I failed to finish my story about hope. Every time I tried my words got stuck, self-conscious and maudlin. The students essays were so compelling I felt I had nothing genuine to add. Hope is the thing with feathers, was that Edna St Vincent Millay? Hope comes in every breath. Inspiration, the perfect word for this unconscious act the ribs moving, lungs filling, heart beating, life flowing in some ancient tide.

Elizabeth Folwell is creative director of Adirondack Life Magazine. *She has been legally blind since September 2001. Her work has appeared in* Gray's Sporting Journal, The New York Times Travel Section, National Geographic Traveler, *and other publications.*

PART TWO

Face Value

Disability Overcome

Face Value
Terry Healey

It was a beautiful Saturday in September 1985, and my friends and I were preparing for a big party we'd be hosting that evening. Late that afternoon, and after numerous cold beers, a group of us wandered out to the courtyard from the inside bar to get some fresh air. Pretty soon, we were all heckling one other and started giving each other short jabs to the shoulders and chest, all in fun. I went for the takedown and knocked my buddy Chip down onto the concrete, where we began wrestling and rolling around.

All of a sudden, blood started trickling out of my nose. I wasn't overly surprised because I'd had frequent nosebleeds throughout my life.

"Oh, dude, I'm sorry," Chip said, helping me up. "I didn't mean to hit your nose."

"Don't worry. It's no big deal," I said.

But suddenly I wasn't interested in horsing around anymore. The bleeding was getting heavier, and what scared me was that I didn't remember him hitting me in the nose at all. I covered my nose and mouth with my hands and ran up to my room. I dashed to the sink, turned on the cold water, and splashed water over my face.

The bleeding stopped almost immediately, but when I looked in the mirror, I felt my stomach cramp in panic. I could see an ivory-colored lump sticking up from the lower section of my right nostril. It seemed as if the bleeding was coming from that area. This didn't seem like my run-of-the-mill nosebleed. A year earlier, the doctors had told me that they had gotten rid of all of the cancer. But now, I started wondering. Had it come back?

●

It had all begun a year earlier, in Berkeley, California, on a sunny but chilly Saturday morning in October 1984. I was twenty and a junior majoring in political science at the University of California at Berkeley, commonly known as "Cal." I was president of the Zeta Phi fraternity, also known as the Zete House, a fraternity more famous for its parties than for its members' academic achievements.

My mother, father, and three brothers were all on hand for the big game between the California Golden Bears and the University of Southern California Trojans at Memorial Stadium. My mother was treasurer of the Zete mothers club, which was putting on a fundraising luncheon as the mothers did every year. It would be a joyful day with plenty of food and drink.

It would also be the day that an offhand remark by my oldest brother Steve would change my life forever.

I got up at about ten, in plenty of time for the start of the festivities at eleven, when we would start serving beer, wine, and gin fizzes to Zete alumni, friends, parents, and ourselves. As president, I was obligated to be on the scene to greet everyone. My brother Steve, who had also been a Zete at Cal several years earlier, knocked on my door just before eleven. While I was getting dressed, we brought each other up to date on what we had been up to. I had the Cal marching band album cranking on my stereo, trying to energize myself and everyone who could hear it into believing that Cal's football team could actually win this game.

I gave myself a final look in the mirror, then turned to face him. "I'm ready to go."

Steve squinted at me. "Hey, Terry, what's going on with your nose?"

"What?"

"Take a look. Your right nostril looks like it's flared out."

"What are you talking about?" I went back to the mirror and took a look. He was right. I had never noticed it, but my right nostril did look bigger than the left one. "Well, it's probably nothing," I shrugged. "Let's go grab a gin fizz."

Two weeks later I stood in line at Sproul Hall, the Cal administration building, to pick up my new picture student identification card. When I reached the front of the line, a cute and cheerful girl asked for my last name.

"Healey," I said.

She searched through her box of alphabetized, plastic coated cards, and without even asking for the actual spelling, pulled out my card quickly.

"Here you go," she said, not taking even a second to look at the picture beside my name. She was the perfect candidate for a job like this—a smile that wouldn't quit despite the monotony of her task.

"Thank you," I said. Before stepping away, I looked at the card to examine it and make sure all the information was correct. But my picture caught my eye. There was no doubt it was me, but I had to take a closer look at the photo. The distortion on the right side of my nose was so obvious, I couldn't believe I hadn't noticed it shaving or brushing my teeth every morning.

I finally made an appointment with a doctor, who performed a biopsy.

It turned out that I had a tumor—a rare fibrosarcoma. My doctor said I'd need follow-up surgery to excise any tumor cells left behind after the biopsy. I wasn't alarmed, and the surgery proved to be minor. With only a few sutures alongside my nose and a few more inside my palate, I returned to classes looking like I had been in a fight with someone, not something. I fell back into my old patterns—procrastinating about my upcoming midterms and term papers, and even hanging out in those same Berkeley bars.

But, six months later, I had the nose bleed and discovered a new lump rising from the lower portion of my right nostril. Then, a tingling in my cheek. Visits to numerous specialists confirmed that my previously unthreatening tumor had become a potentially disfiguring, life-threatening malignancy. My doctor informed me that I could lose half my nose, half my upper lip, and possibly my right eye, but that saving my life was his main concern. The realization that I could be disfigured was devastating.

I awoke from the first surgery with a skin graft attached to my face that used skin and fat from my shoulder and chest. Half of my nose and my upper lip were gone. The muscle and bone from my right cheek had been excised. The shelf of my eye, six teeth, and part of my hard palate had been removed. My doctor promised to make me "streetable" before I left the hospital. I assumed that must have meant "acceptable". I imagined that "streetable" might mean looking like Tom Berenger did in *Platoon*, a 1985 Vietnam War film, where he had a big, thick keloid scar across his cheek as a result of a knife wound he had received in battle. I could live with that. It might even improve my chances with girls. I could don a "tough guy" look, and maybe even broaden my appeal. I later realized that "streetable" was my doctor's term for preparing me for a life of disfigurement.

I had two more procedures to remove the remaining malignancy, and then I was released from the hospital. That's when I began to realize the severity of my situation. Inside the hospital, I had been protected and insulated. Outside of it, I was vulnerable and exposed. Upon leaving the hospital, I noticed adults staring at me. Children pointed and sometimes laughed. One woman's jaw dropped in shock and horror.

How was I going to face the world? I cared what other people thought of me. I relished the admiring looks I had received as the "old Terry" and was petrified of the reaction I'd get to the "new Terry." Over the next few months, the inadvertently negative reactions and comments I sometimes received left an indelible mark on me. Meanwhile, radiation treatments had begun to shrink the tissue on my face, magnifying my deformity. My self-esteem sank lower than I thought possible. I found myself constantly seeking reassurance from people.

Did my looks bother them? What did they see? Did they like me? How could they like me? I was still coping with the insecurity after five years and twenty attempts to reconstruct my face.

When I had my last reconstructive procedure, I met a woman who was also being treated at the hospital. We began dating. One day, after I had asked her, for the umpteenth time, how she felt about my looks, she ripped into me. The bulk of my problem, she said, was not my physical appearance, but my emotional insecurity. Her honesty helped me realize that surgery would not fix the mental and emotional scars that had become far more disfiguring than the appearance of my face.

I began to examine myself from the inside out. The support of family and friends, prayer, and the realization that my scars were deeper on the inside than the outside collectively strengthened my spirit and my belief in myself. I ended my quest to find the next wizard surgeon who would miraculously repair my eye, rebuild my nose, or rebuild my upper lip so that I could regain my smile of yesteryear. Instead, I began volunteering at The Wellness Community, a cancer support organization that offers hope and support for cancer patients and their families. Helping others proved to be the best therapy. I began to feel better about myself as I realized that I could bring tremendous inspiration and hope to others coping with cancer. Each week after attending meetings at The Wellness Community, I began to rebuild my confidence and belief in self. For the first time, I felt like I was taking two steps forward and one step back, instead of the other way around. Over time, the pain I felt from being an outcast subsided.

Shortly thereafter, I met Sue, who is today my wife. We had two dates before she even asked me what had happened to me. That told me a lot about Sue. She really wasn't concerned about what happened to me. She cared about who I was as a person. Finding Sue and opening up to her proved to be my most significant turning point. She accepted me for who I was, and to this day has not asked me to change.

Perhaps I will always be a kind of outcast, but it's not pain that I feel any more. I'm thankful for who I am today—much stronger and wiser than I was before cancer and the disfigurement associated with it. We all struggle with insecurities in one form or another. For me, it took something devastating – something that would take me to the depths of self-evaluation—to realize that battle scars are what make people interesting. Battle scars are what make people wise. Battle scars are what make people realize how precious and valuable life really is. Battle scars are what prepare people for the inevitable adversity that lies ahead.

Nineteen years after my last radiation treatment, I remain cancer-free. I've accomplished a lot personally and professionally. I published a book about my experience, called *At Face Value*. One of the most therapeutic outcomes of the book's release has been the opportunity I've had to speak to groups of cancer patients, medical professionals, businesses, associations, and students. I learned a lot at a very young age and am grateful for those gifts and lessons, which I hope to share with people facing challenges and adversity in their own lives. One of my goals today is to help others to become more tolerant. Regardless of the color of our skin, our sexual orientation, the shape of our bodies, or the imperfections of our faces, we all need to remember that it is the internal, and not the external fabric that makes up our human spirit.

Terry Healey is a technology marketing strategy consultant. He is also an author and a motivational speaker. You can contact him via email at terry@terryhealey. com. For more information about his speaking and his recently released book, At Face Value: My Triumph Over A Disfiguring Cancer, *please visit his website www.terryhealey.com.*

A Seminoma Story
Nathan Abrams

Testicular cancer is one of those things that I thought would never happen to me. It only happens to about 2000 men per year in the United Kingdom, where I live. For years my mother asked if my I checked myself regularly. I replied only somewhat jokingly that I checked the shaft part extremely frequently. Then, when my then-girlfriend moved from the United States to London, she started telling me that one of my testicles was bigger than the other. My response to that was that they only look that way because one hangs lower so that they don't bash when you walk. However, while cycling, I noticed that things weren't hanging quite right. I thought this was down to my choice of baggy clothing. But when I took a bath, I noticed that my left testicle had swollen to the size of a lemon (as compared to the walnut shape of the other one) and was harder than the right one. At this point, I knew something was wrong and slowly began to feel very scared. I got out of the bath and rang my General Practitioner immediately. When I explained the problem to his receptionist I got an immediate appointment. Half an hour later I had my trousers and underpants down in front of the doctor and he without delay referred me, as a matter of urgency, to the Royal Free Hospital in North London for further tests.

Ten days later, on a Friday afternoon, after some questions and prodding, a consultant urologist ascertained that I had a testicular swelling/tumour but of what kind he wouldn't say. He sent me down for an immediate ultrasound and arranged for me to have a series of blood tests and an X-Ray. It was only on the following Monday when I was back in hospital for more tests that I was told—for the first time—that I had cancer; up until that point, no one had used the dreaded "C-word."

It all came so fast that I didn't really have time to think about it. On reflection, though, as Lance Armstrong put it in his autobiography, "Anyone who has heard the words, You have cancer has thought, Oh, my God, I'm going to die." But at the time, I was distracted by the series of blood tests I was required to have, one of which was for HIV (in line with European Union directives). For two hours I worried that the result could be positive (if only 45% of all testicular lumps are cancer then isn't there a small chance I have AIDS, too?). As the minutes ticked by, I got increasingly nervous and stressed about the results of my AIDS test. The cancer was at the back of my mind. Finally, I was informed that my test was negative. Despite the relief, I was physically exhausted and emotionally drained.

When you're diagnosed with cancer, things begin to move very quickly as the surgeons want to remove the tumour as soon as possible. The day after my diagnosis I was scheduled for surgery. On that same day, I "banked" sperm in case anything went wrong during surgery or afterwards and I want to be able to father kids in the future. In the afternoon, I was admitted to hospital. The following morning, I was taken down for surgery. It was all a bit of a whirlwind. Although I felt a little nervous before the surgery, I was also relieved. The wait was over and the tumour was to be removed. In the pre-op area, the surgeon came into say hello and asked if the testicle had been marked. I replied that it hadn't but assured him that since it was so huge he couldn't miss it even if he tried. "That," he replied, "is why we're so worried." He then rushed around looking for a marker pen and when he finally located one he drew a large purple arrow on my leg, indicating the testicle to remove. This is done to ensure the right bit is removed and so reduce the number of mistakes in surgery. The procedure I was to undergo, known as a radical orchidectomy, required my left groin area to be shaved, an incision made, and the whole testis and tumour removed while the spertal cord is cauterised. All the time, the surgeon is very careful to reduce the possibility that cancer cells are transported in the blood to elsewhere in my body.

The tumour turned out to be a "classic seminoma"(Greek for testicular tumour). I was told that if given a choice then this would be the kind of cancer to choose as it is non-aggressive and very responsive to treatment with a 98% rate of effectiveness. Furthermore, it was at Stage 1 which meant that the cancer was confined to the testis and had not spread to anywhere else in my body (the big worry for those diagnosed with cancer).

Although the tumour had been removed and the cancer had not spread, my treatment had not ended. Now referred to the Oncology Unit at the Royal Free, I was given a choice of post-surgery treatments: either ten days of prophylactic "dog-leg" radiotherapy to wipe out any possible remaining cancer cells and reduce the chance of a relapse to roughly 2% or "active surveillance" involving regular, monthly check ups and X-Rays and blood tests and a Computer Tomography (CT) scan every three months. Because of the (embarrassing, in my opinion) size of my tumour (75 mm x 45 mm x 32 mm), the oncologists estimated my chance of a relapse as 30-40% (approximately 10% higher than in normal sized cases). I chose the active surveillance option, but after only two months I received the bad news that a routine CT scan showed an enlarged lymph node which meant that the cancer had spread. Because my secondary (Stage IIa) cancer was at such an early stage of development, I was given a choice of systemic chemotherapy or localised, targeted radiotherapy. I chose the latter because, never having been really ill before, I couldn't comprehend how chemo (which can be very aggressive) physically breaks a person down just to destroy one small tiny cancerous growth. I felt fine: fit, well and healthy. In fact, I was then probably in the best shape of my life. I also did not want to lose my fine head of hair. As Melanie McFadyean wrote, "You cannot imagine what it is like losing your hair, nor overestimate its visceral horror."

In the meantime, I returned to the fertility clinic several times, banking more sperm as a precautionary measure. Sperm banking is the preservation of sperm by freezing so that they may be used subsequently for artificial in-semination or other assisted reproduction techniques, as two possible effects of radiotherapy are: that no sperms will be present after the therapy or that therapy will have the potential to affect the DNA of the sperm. I am told to return one year after the end of the radiotherapy treatment to produce another sample for analysis.

Overall, in the Lab Assistant's words, my results were "very good." I had above average amount, count and motility (the ability to move spontaneously and independently) is 60% (normal is 40%). I filled thirteen vials, each of which is enough for to create one pregnancy.

Needless to say, I felt rather pleased with my performance in the midst of all the worry.

Radiotherapy treatment took place once every working day for seventeen days so three and a half weeks in total. It took this long because an overall dose was worked out but administered partially in order to give my healthy cells and tissue time to recover. Also, if administered all in one go, it would have been intolerable and as it was the side effects were most unpleasant anyway.

Treatment involved being positioned very precisely on a bench by several radiographers who talked numbers as if putting up shelves. Three dots had previously been permanently tattooed in a line on the skin on either side of my waist and below my belly button so they could line up the X-rays which were beamed to the area of my abdomen known as the para-aortic region and which contained the lymph nodes either side of my spine. Vital organs and my healthy testis were protected by a specially and specifically designed high-density alloy mould which was fitted to the X-ray machine (which itself looked like a giant camera lens). I was not allowed to help as they moved me about. Incongruous pop music played in the background but it was more distracting than relaxing. Once positioned correctly, the radiographers bolted out of the room. I was zapped for several minutes during which time I had to lie very still. The machine was then rotated so I could be zapped from below in order to get both sides of me.

It was very peculiar to be treated in this way because it didn't feel like anything was done to me, that is, there were no needles, anaesthetics, incisions, or so on. The whole treatment was practically invisible. I didn't feel nor smell anything: the only reason I knew I was being X-rayed was because the radiographers left the room and the machine made a whirring noise. It was also strange being left in a closed, windowless room, behind thick, reinforced walls, alone with material too dangerous for anyone else to be present.

Compared to chemotherapy, I'm sure radiotherapy is a cakewalk. Yet, I can say that it is not pleasant neither physically nor psychologically and I'm still glad that when offered a choice between radiotherapy and active surveillance back in January that I opted for the latter. I still see no need to put oneself through a radiotherapy regime unless absolutely necessary. Radiotherapy affects everyone differently but my side effects included dehydration, diarrhoea, stomach cramps, wind, tiredness, weight loss, mental boredom and monotony, skin irritation, dryness, soreness itchiness and hair loss in the affected area only. The main side effect was nausea. Although I was given anti-nausea pills, these weren't entirely effective against irradiating such a large area of my bowels and intestines, and I threw up twice on my first day of treatment. I was also slowly being emasculated: I had lost a testicle, my sperm were killed (temporarily I hope), I had enlarged breasts, and, I was reliably informed by my female friends, that I exhibited all the symptoms of a having a period. Fortunately, my daily fix of a cocktail of pills did the trick, and eventually I began to approach male normality once again.

My radiotherapy treatment was considered to be "definitive." I am now deemed "unremarkable." In oncology terms, this is a good thing, as it means I am cancer-free. Nonetheless, as the UK's national protocol for the treatment of cancer dictates, I still have to be checked regularly for the next ten years although the gap between appointments grows bigger as the years progress.

Although one testicle down, I function just as well on one as most men do on two, if not better, as evidenced by my above average sperm count. Besides, men are designed, just like airplanes, to function on one engine. The only real difference is aesthetics and to be honest, I don't really look very different from before. Yes, I have a bit of excess skin, resembling a bulldog's neck, but this is hardly noticeable and the other testis has dropped into the middle occupying the recently-vacated space, and apparently, although I can't tell, has increased in size to compensate for the loss. I was offered a prosthetic free of charge on the National Health Service but I didn't want to have to go through another surgical procedure.

The scar from surgery is almost invisible and the tattooed dots are very hard to locate. I also have the option of having them removed by laser should I wish but since I can't see them I've decided not to. I suppose they are also a "memento" of my experiences. Nonetheless, I feel more streamlined especially now that I've gotten rid of the tumescent testis and the deadweight has been excised to my eternal benefit. Also, the cancer should not affect my long-term chances of having kids.

How did cancer change me? I once thought that expressions of sympathy were formulaic and meaningless. Cancer made me realise that such expressions are very important to those listening. Words, any words, even if they are not our own really do help. Their absence is hurtful. Unfortunately, it is at times like these that one finds out who one's friends are and I was hurt by those friends, colleagues, and acquaintances who had nothing at all whatsoever to say about my illness. I learned that a large part of being alive is the feeling of being loved and of loving. This is part of the reason why visiting people in hospital is so important.

I have also become more self-aware. For example, apart from recognising and acknowledging my emotions, I also know that my sperm is healthy and that I am HIV free. These are things I did not know before the onset of my cancer. The strange thing is, now that I've had both surgery and radiotherapy treatment, I am probably or possibly as healthy as a healthy person, if not even healthier in that I am being checked monthly for potential relapse while they are not. Indeed, according to John Diamond, it can take a cancer cell three years to grow to a size where it becomes noticeable, and further, by that point, the cancer is already 75% through its lifespan. The other weird thing is that if it does take cancer three years to grow, it means I've had it since sometime in 2000. Actually, in a sense, I've always had it, as cancer is essentially a disease whereby one cell fails to obey its genetic instructions to die and (as Diamond put it) then tells its friends the secret of immortality. The irony is that cancer relies on the body to survive and grow but in doing so kills the very thing keeping it alive in the first place.

Looking back one year after my initial discovery, those around me were more shocked by the whole experience than I was. Don't get me wrong, I was very scared at times during my experience but cancer of any sort is a real shock to others. Among my friends in particular, I was the "healthy" one, who ate properly, exercised regularly, and never got ill and once I was diagnosed I sprang the whole thing on them very suddenly. Because it was "cancer," many people were worried on my behalf (as McFadyean put it so eloquently, "When people hear you have cancer, they foresee a death foretold"), and I had friends and family on several continents praying for my well-being, including some who hadn't said a prayer in decades. Had I wanted to, though, I probably could have kept the whole thing from them, as seminoma can be discovered, diagnosed, and treated very quickly and before there are any outward signs visible to other people. In fact, because of the localised nature of the cancer, early detection means that recovery rate after surgery with no need for further surgery is approximately 98%.

Now, with the cancer behind me, it is funny how something that was once so scary is now just a part of my past and how my fears at the time did not reflect the reality of the situation in any way.

Nathan Abrams teaches Film Studies at the University of Wales, Bangor, UK. He was diagnosed with cancer in 2003 and received treatment until June 2004. He has since then been considered oncologically healthy. His latest book is Commentary Magazine 1945-1959: "A journal of significant thought and opinion" (*Vallentine Mitchell, 2006*).

To the Summit or Bust
Eileen Rudnick

I watched from a distance as she walked toward me. Her progress was un-hurried. I seemed to be standing still, but I wasn't sure. I did not feel anything under my feet. The surrounding soft, green light captured my attention. We were in a garden, the likes of which is not seen except in dreams. Exceedingly tall plants grew up around us. Some of the plants were topped with vivid blos-soms far out of reach. The woman and I existed at root level, like ants, but we were alone in this quiet, peaceful place. The verdant scent reminded me of pleasurable moments in my grandfather's garden, lying on my back between the rows. I remembered precisely spaced stalks of corn touching the sky, a hedge-row of lacy carrot tops, and determined green peas drooping under the weight of heavy pods. Statuesque hollyhocks stood together like grand dames in color-ful gowns. Although I was happily five years old again, I turned my attention back to the woman. The light chestnut-brown hair, greenish eyes, and freckled skin were very familiar. She was small, but womanly. When her sunny regard washed over me, I was excited to acknowledge the presence of my restored mother. The youthful, vibrant woman is proof of what will happen to me upon my death, I thought. My mind, body, and soul will be reunited when I die. Moreover, even if some of the parts are broken, damaged, or diseased, the sum of my whole person will be fresh and new. I know this to be true, because my mother died three years previously, withered, with a few tufts of white hair, and delirious from morphine for the pain of cancer. This must be how she looked in her youth, which I don't remember.

On another level, the trauma team moved quickly and expertly over the mangled mess of a woman lying helplessly unconscious before them. I had arrived by helicopter moments before, after being extracted from a twisted wreck. Just one hour ago, I had been driving home from work. Now my life was on hold and my survival in question. The excitement of my new job with a significant raise in salary was already over, and I would never return. The trauma specialist made a careful examination of my unconscious form, noting my numerous injuries. He was very concerned about the evident internal hemorrhage, therefore, had me in emergency surgery within an hour of my arrival. He successfully found and repaired liver lacerations, and even though there was significant loss of blood, I survived. I did not awaken after surgery, however. I remained in a coma for about five days, due to the brain injury, and I would never be the same. While my scared and desperate family watched and waited, I continued to spend time in an enchanted garden with my late mother. As she came close to me, I marveled at the strong resemblance between us. We did not touch. Instead, my mother extended her slim hand toward me in a gesture not to come any closer. She said with strength and conviction, "You can't stay. You have to go back. You still have too much work to do." I don't know if I answered, but that was the end of our time together. My husband has reported to me that one of my earliest queries when I became conscious, was which hospital room did my mother have.

My actual return to consciousness happened about three weeks before my memory resumed. Regaining a fully functioning memory is a slow, tough climb up a mountain, with frequent slips backward. One of my earliest achievements was the ability to stay awake for more than five minutes at a time. There were spoon-feedings by my husband, hospital staff getting me out of bed and holding me steady on my feet for a few steps, and my family and staff constantly cueing me to keep me oriented to place and time. I was taken for rides in wheelchairs, and propped up in front of windows. All this and much more does not exist in my memory. I have yet to discover the comfort in amnesia some individuals tell me I should have. By the time my memory was fully functional, I had already relearned walking, talking, eating, personal care, reading, writing, and math. Some may conclude that my story ends there, but I can tell you that I am still on the lowest slopes of Mount Everest.

There is not one aspect of myself unaffected by brain injury. I am still struggling with recovery from and residual effects of dual disability: physical and emotional. My appearance is deceptive. Aside from scars, evidence of disability is not visible. The damaged and disconnected axons in my brain do not show when I struggle to comprehend a sewing pattern. Behaviors and conversations of others seem to be at light speed, compared to my donkey-cart processing speed.Innuendo and subtlety are wasted on me. I don't always get it. I can usually handle direct communication, without too many layers of information. Problem solving is no longer my forte. My effort, too often, does not progress beyond restating the problem over and over again in my brain.

I can even become confused trying to keep all of my signs and symptoms straight. When I sob uncontrollably, is it labile emotions or depression? When

I burp loudly in a restaurant, is it because I am uninhibited, or is it just gas? When I ask the gum-chewing clerk on the phone, who has messed up another form, which one of us has the brain injury, is it misplaced anger or self-advocacy? When I'm terrified of the traffic, even as a passenger, is it post-traumatic stress disorder, even though I have amnesia? When I'm the only one who laughs out loud, is it immaturity or am I in a better mood? When I'm disappointed because a friend doesn't understand me, is it an unreasonable expectation? Is heightened libido due to more acute senses, being uninhibited, or am I an immoral old bird? Have I become irresponsible because I tend to live for today? So many questions with a wide assortment of answers—because brain injury is not definitive either.

Years ago, when I became an accountant, I thought that I had found a perfect match for my strengths and talents. I was precise and detail-oriented. I could sort through a tall, messy stack of paperwork and computer printouts littering my desk, and convert it into a neat, thorough and informative report to present at a finance meeting in the morning. I worked long hours into the evening and on weekends. My life revolved around spreadsheets, account analysis, journal entries, production costs, and inventory levels. I was sharp and determined to learn anything anyone cared to teach me. My bosses marveled at the quantity and quality of work I produced. That person was lost in a car wreck in October 2000.

For the last four and a half years, my energy has been focused on the arduous journey upward from coma. I have divided my recovery thus far into three layers, building a step ladder.

In the beginning, there was emergence. In this stage I was tender, uninformed, apathetic, untrained, and bewildered. I equate this stage with babyhood, complete with needed boundaries, within which I felt secure. My days were spent in my favorite chair, cared for by my husband, surrounded by books for reading and notebooks for writing. I did not answer the phone or the door. All my activities were arranged by my husband, and I only left the house for therapy. I have vague memories of this time, as the shock of traumatic brain injury was still fresh. This stage lasted about one year. There is no clear cut-off, however. It was just the beginning of an accelerated maturation process that continues. Books borrowed from the library were on the following subjects: brain function, brain injury, personal stories about brain injury, and SAT tutorials. It was a heavy assortment for someone less than one year out of coma. A statement gleaned from one of these "expert" theorists caused me more emotional trauma. He suggested that after one year of recovery, I would be as good as I was going to be. The first anniversary of the incident was a black hole for me. During this time I required one mid-day nap, and still went to bed early. During the day, I journalized and wrote short essays about my experience - calling them "scenarios." I do not know where I got the word; I just liked the way it sounded.

Step two was reflection. I was curious, eager, sad, angry, yearning, volatile, and self-obsessed. I continued to read books about brain injury, and compared these to my own records—in the absence of memory—but comprehension was still elusive. I felt disconnected from myself because of amnesia. I was still secretly convinced that whatever was wrong with me was temporary. I was impatient for it to end, so that I could get back to what I was doing. Sometimes my frustration erupted into extreme anger or deep despair and tearfulness. I was unaware of many of my cognitive and emotional deficits, especially self-control, and my self-obsession was pathological. Every idea, conclusion, and action of me or others was related to my brain injury. I said the phrase "brain damaged" constantly to myself, and very unkindly. Shame and embarrassment were having serious effects on me. I cried copiously just because I felt so bad, and I didn't know why. I had not started to come to terms with my disability. I read about cognitive deficits, but I did not want to believe that I had any. Most of my grief and anger seemed to result from a feeling of being punished for reasons unknown. I wanted to vent my wrath on whoever allowed this injustice to happen. The second anniversary came and went, and I began to yearn for something different.

The third level is exploration. This stage is exciting, educational, inspirational, exhausting, frightening, and therapeutic. My days are full of exercise for my body and mind, volunteering in the brain injury community, and family enjoyment. Stepping away from self-imposed isolation was terrifying, and I needed my husband's strong support to do it. I was not happy when I was avoiding the world, but my anxiety level is much higher now. Manifestations of my brain injury are fully exposed to public scrutiny. When I become aware that some of my deficits are revealed, I feel humiliated and defiant at the same time. I sometimes wonder if my extreme self-consciousness is entirely under my control. Whatever happened to the strong, self-confident woman who could rise up at high level meetings, holding her own and scared of nothing? My desire to learn more about this new world in which I exist, however, is much stronger than my anxiety. So I continue, but sometimes I am completely exhausted. I no longer require a midday nap, but I am usually in bed early—sometimes by 9pm.

In a typical day, you may engage in multitasking, problem solving, prioritizing a long list of tasks, and retiring at the end of the day, tired, but satisfied with your accomplishments. You even find the energy, somehow, to repeat it after a short rest. For a brain injured survivor, to face such a day once in a while is manageable. To try to do it several days in a row may yield dramatic re-sults. Dizziness, slurred speech, marked clumsiness, lower level cognitive abili-ties, crankiness or over emotion are just some of the possibilities. I sometimes need a few days to recover from such exhaustion. Since I must take my brain injury with me, the burden can feel like the chains on Jacob Marley's ghost in *A Christmas Carol*. I can only complete a much smaller list of tasks than I used to, and I am not always content about it. My more frequent errors are even harder to accept.

During the time spent volunteering at The Brain Injury Association of Maryland, I have acquired much more knowledge of my disability than that with which I arrived. I have become acquainted with many injured survi-vors with whom I share similar experiences, issues and symptoms. I am not alone. There are millions of us, and I take comfort in that fact. I also derive a huge amount of pleasure in service of others like me. I am still incredulous when another injured survivor tells me that I have been a big help. I am the one who just a couple of years ago didn't think that I would ever be useful again. Now I am inspired to keep on trying. Why did I never notice that people helping people is the finest tool we possess? When one of my associates kindly takes the time to remind me to eat, I now realize that I am experiencing caring, not a superior intellect.

The significant life change that happened to me has left me still shocked and traumatized. I know that I can never go back; therefore I feel mournful regret, but so much more in addition. As if my senses have been scrubbed, they now deliver pure information to my brain. When I gaze out the window and see colors more vivid than I ever noticed before, I am inspired to go out-side. Once outside, I notice many layers of scents and levels of sounds. I like the sensation of fresh air on my skin and in my lungs. I say a prayer of thanks for living and feeling.

A long walk is an excellent opportunity for drawing inward to contemplate the many questions that still haunt me. The rhythmic pounding of my feet on the pavement can be meditative. Sometimes I return from a walk with answers. Walking is one of the many forms of exercise from which I derive the extremely pleasurable feeling of wellness. Teaching my body the way to become stronger is a powerful stimulant.

Exploration can lead to discovery. It is thrilling to look around and no-tice that everything seems fresh and new. Boredom does not exist for me any-more, and what a wonderful surprise to discover that my skills and abilities, although different, are of value. I have found a home in the brain injury com-munity, discovering that there is advantage in being a survivor. The delivery of information about services available from someone on the inside seems especially meaningful to my friends in disability. If my existence can symbolize hope and possibilities, then let it be. I tend to believe that when it comes to the human brain, anything is possible. When I consider my late mother's implied advice, I wonder if I am doing it. Perhaps this is the work to which she was referring.

I have experienced a phenomenon which I call "power surge." I started a project, and almost immediately realized that badly needed and explicit instructions had faded with age; they were unusable. At first I felt a rush of panic. The project was very important to me, and I did not want to waste the raw materials. After several minutes of contemplation, the solution came to me clearly and completely. I had invented an improvisation that worked beautifully to complete the project! I was very excited and proud of this creative problem solving. I even imagined the inner workings of my brain's little axons reaching around a damaged area, like a detour, and successfully finding another route to the same destination. I think that I experienced a kind of "neuro-flexibility." What do you think? Sadly, this phenomenon stands alone, but I am hopeful of adding to the collection.

From time to time in my recovery, I slip into deep despair, too. Occasionally, I have raised an angry voice to God, asking, "Why did you spare me?" I do not always know where this darkness comes from, but I seem to be especially vulnerable. Do you want to know how I escape from the darkness? Well, I cannot do it alone. The following course works best for me:

a. professional counseling

b. loving support from family

c. caring support from associates and friends, and

d. self-determination.

What is self-determination? I find quiet times to get in touch with the person inside me. She is, invariably, serene and content just to be, and sometimes has answers to some of my most troubling questions. With renewed peace and vigor, I can fight for a more tenacious hold on the side of the mountain. Then, like a little flower, the face of my granddaughter captivates me. The wonder and innocence of her expression makes me want to think like her. I never get tired of watching her work. Tiny hands grasp and pick up objects which she then scrutinizes with serious blue eyes. Sometimes her focus is so deep, that a small frown appears on her flawless face. As she thinks baby thoughts and works hard to understand the world, she exhibits peaceful contentment just to be. To hold her little body next to mine is inexpressible joy. Then I thank God for sparing me.

Climbing the mountain is the hardest work I've ever done, but I'm neck to neck with The Little Engine That Could.

The author is a seven-year survivor of TBI. She spends her time serving the brain injury community as a volunteer. Her hobbies are writing, sewing, walking, and working out at the gym. With assistance from her husband of thiry-five years, she runs a brain injury support group near her home.

No Sorrows Will Last Forever
Grace Susanti

May 1998, Jakarta.

"Cewek Cina turun—Chinese women get out!" bellowed a bellicose muscular man, wearing a black T-Shirt and worn-out blue jeans. Sensing danger, I ducked down behind the passenger sitting one row in front of me, and tried to cringe my forehead to the knees. Because this crowded public Metrobus was narrow between each row, my attempt to disappear from his hostile glare failed. Hearing his heavy boots thumping the bus floor towards the rear of the bus, I held my breath. But the sound of my heartbeat drove me crazy. Holding my breath for 300 seconds was possible. Suppressing my heartbeat was very unlikely, even if you were a Houdini or a David Copperfield. Suddenly, he grabbed my waist-long hair: "Sundel, turun lu—get out, you slut." His glassy red eyes did not show any emotion, cold as a dead fish's eyes. Then he kicked my butt, hissing: "Quick. Out!"

What happened to me on that infamous day, Thursday, around 5:30 pm 14th May 1998, on the curb side of Jelambar Road in West Jakarta was beyond civilized human norm. My world turned upside down, in less than an hour.

●

Leaving the UNTAR—Universitas Tarumanegara—medical faculty complex at Grogol thirty minutes earlier, I was the envy of my classmates. Why? I was going to sit in for the final State Medical examination in a fortnight, to be precise in eleven calendar days. It was going to be the last hurdle before pocketing the coveted degree—a Doctor title bestowed upon a medical student with a diploma officially stamped by the influential State Tertiary Education Department. All marginalized medical students—mostly Chinese Indonesian—from non-government funded private universities had to wait patiently for this formal State examination. In my case, two and a half years. Then a month later, the wedding. Wedding in June, my girlhood's wish. We would have a big family. Four kids at least. I love children so much. "Two, a boy and a girl, are enough," said Robby, smiling. At twenty-six I had a rosy future. Rob, my fiancé, also twenty-six had just started his internship. Later we planned to take the ECFMG exam for foreign medical graduates, the first step to enter America prior to obtaining the Green Card. The dream to live and work in a country where honey and milk flow on the streets would come true. A land with limitless opportunities.

As a grateful daughter, the youngest among four siblings, I had been planning since my high school years to make my parents happy during their twilight years. I would work hard and save money to buy them a decent house. They deserved better than just the leaking crowded old ruko-house cum shop, where my father sold plastic ware, soft drinks, mineral water, instant noodles, cooking oil, sugar, soy sauce, flour, salted fish. All sorts of stuffs for the people on the street.

●

"Gang raping Chinese women in broad daylight, then stabbing the victims' vaginas with a corroded iron rod in front of a jeering crowd was only a baseless rumor," declared General Roesmanhadi, Indonesian Police Chief. "Rumor mongers will be charged!" warned the Intelligence Chief, General Moetojib sternly.

With a charming smile, General Wiranto (it was grossly unfair to accuse him of hiding his Schadenfreude on hearing the agony endured by the Chinese girls and women during the mid May 1998 riot preceding the downfall of the thirty-two-year old General Soeharto regime) proclaimed his mendacious statement on national TV, beamed live throughout the archipelago:

"No gang rapes have ever happened in Jakarta. Not a single rape victim has come forward!"

Who dared to refute the statement of the Chief of Staffs and Defense Minister, the No. 1 powerful man in Indonesia, the most populous Muslim country on earth with its 230 million people? Adding insult to injury, Mayor General. Syamsoeddin, Greater Jakarta Military Commander declared that the capital city was safe and under control! What a ludicrous statement!

●

I didn't know the Samaritan, who took my body to the nearest hospital. Regaining consciousness many hours later at Rumah Sakit Sumber Waras in Grogol, I felt throbbing pain in my lower abdomen. I couldn't even lift my legs. I was shocked. I was in denial.

Nothing had happened to me on that roadside, I kept on telling myself: "No, it was only a nightmare. I had to prepare for my final State Medical exam. I got only eleven days left."

One quiet afternoon after the visiting hours were over, lying on my clean hospital bed, watching the downpour through the wide glass window, I remembered reading an ancient saying which I did not fully comprehend at that time. The Korean proverb says: "During our short pilgrimage on earth, each of us will experience ten thousand joys and ten thousand sorrows."

Only a chosen few had to bear this titanic cross: the utmost punishment for a human being, the most degrading humiliation of being gang-raped in front of the jubilant crowd, in front of one very own fellow citizens. To suffer ten thousand sorrows in just one installment, in less than an hour instead of seventy-five years was my fate. I counted myself, and my fellow unfortunate sisters among them. I didn't dare to put any figure on my poor sisters, because our jingoistic, biased local journalists would immediately point out the inaccuracy. Instead of 169, they insisted "only" 168 had been gang-raped including 20 who committed suicide. Only 168 Chinese women and girls. "Only!" How inconsiderate one could be, when reporting the misfortune that had befallen the despised minority.

My perpetrators or most likely, God, had been "merciful" to me. Because of the potential lethal infection inflicted by the penetrating contaminated iron rod, the surgeons removed my ruptured Fallopian tubes. Some of my other sisters were not that "lucky," and had to suffer for their entire lives. They got pregnant.

•

Flight SQ 156 Jakarta-Singapore.

January 1999, Cengkareng Airport, Jakarta.

"Singapore Airline Flight one five six to Singapore is now boarding at Gate 9. Passengers are requested to proceed to ..."

Without waiting for the rest of the flight announcement I dashed to the gate. The airline ground attendant, in a courteous manner stopped me: "Your boarding pass ma'am." I rummaged through my handbag. None. My jacket, none. My jeans' pockets. Empty. The queue was getting longer. Her colleague asked me to step aside to free the bottleneck. Frantically I opened my carry bag. None. Sweat began rolling down my forehead. Why did this thing happen?

At this critical moment, I couldn't wait to leave the land of my tormentors. How could I be so careless. I must have dropped this damned boarding pass, somewhere. Ladies room? In the airport bookshop? I couldn't remember. Blank. I was too occupied, checking my watch every two minutes. Seeing tears start streaming down my cheek, the attendant called her ground supervisor. All passengers had embarked except one. My name was on the passenger list. Five long minutes of discussion amongst the SQ team seemed an eternity to me. Finally, they let me in. I was the last passenger instead of the first to enter flight

SQ 156 to freedom, and hopefully a new life. I will never look back. Never.

My euphoria was short-lived. The plane was full. All eyes stared at me while the gracious flight attendant ushered this last passenger to the only empty seat, 14B. To my horror seats 14A and 14C were occupied by indigenous Indonesian businessmen. Since the fateful day, May 14th 1998, I have never been the same person. I trembled when I saw strong Indonesian men, like a five-year-old docile kid summoned by the strict Kindergarten teacher—awaiting punishment. Should I be punished when my only "crime" was being born as a female Chinese minority?

Regaining my composure after thinking that this 100-minute flight would soon be over, I hesitantly took my seat.

•

My two neighbors were trying to strike a small chat by asking intrusive questions. "Sendirian aja Dik—travelling alone little sister? Suaminya jaga rumah ya—your husband minding the house?" They finally got tired when I did not respond to their harassment. The one on my left grumbled: "Bisu kali—mute girl." The flight was full of Chinese Indonesian tourists who were visiting China, their ancestral land. They did not bother to speak Indonesian. I did not understand their loud conversation, maybe in Mandarin or Hokkien or Cantonese or Teochew.

I overheard the stinging remark from the one on my right: "Dasar Cina, ngga mau ngomong Indonesia. Nanti kalu diperkosa lagi, rasain lu!" (These damned Chinese! Refusing to speak Indonesian. Being raped again will make them come to their senses!) How could someone curse others, full of hatred, without a gram of empathy in his heart? Hearing the word "rape" reminded me of my agony eight months ago.

I bit my lower lip hard to suppress my emotion. I felt salt on the tip of my tongue. The red-stained handkerchief sent shivers down my spine. I could not help myself. I burst into tears.

•

QF Flight 78 Singapore-Perth.

Feeling thirsty, I stumbled down the aisle towards the rear of the aircraft looking for a glass of water. Cruising at 33,000 feet over the Indian Ocean, halfway between Singapore and Perth most of the passengers were asleep during this five-hour, 3,000-kilometer flight, except a few who were still reading. I could not locate the cold-water dispenser when I heard a confident voice, "Can I get you some water, ma'am?"

"Yee..es eer please," I stammered. To my astonishment, the voice came from a flight attendant who did not look like a Caucasian. However, her English did sound as if she were a native speaker.

"Are you Chinese?"

Luckily, she did not regard that question as a rude one coming from a bad mannered person. Smiling she answered, "No, I am an Australian."

I envied the confident tone in her voice pronouncing the word 'Australian' without any slightest hesitation at all. To pronounce such a short sentence with pride and confidence, "I am an Indonesian," would never happen to me during my twenty-seven years living in my birth country as a minority. With my heavy Betawi accent, I tried to practice my English by asking her several unintelligent questions such as: where her hometown was, how many years with Qantas and how could a minority get a job with a national carrier.

'Fiona Chang' stood on her nametag. One hundred and fifty years ago her great-great-grandfather fled the impoverished Fujian province in Southern China to better his living by working in the goldfields of Ballarat, 105 km Northwest of Melbourne, where they suffered discriminations and violent physical abuses by the "pure" true-blue xenophobic gold miners. Now she and her fifth-generation family called Brisbane their home.

Out of curiosity I asked her how could she, as a Chinese Australian got a flight attendant job with Qantas, formerly known as Queensland and Northern Territory Air Services, a semi-national carrier. She gave me an incredulous look for asking such a dumb question.

"You lost me. Every Australian regardless of their ethnic background can apply for any job with the government. You get the job if you meet the job requirements."

She was a bit confused after hearing that not a single Chinese Indonesian woman had ever been employed as flight attendant by Garuda Airways, the Indonesian national carrier.

"Haven't heard about this before," she murmured.

"By the way, my name is Grace Susanti," I introduced myself voluntarily.

"You know mine," smiling, she pointed with her right thumb to the nametag on her left breast." Susanti, Susanti, let me refresh my memory, ah you must be related to Susi Susanti the legendary four-time All England Woman Single Champion and the Barcelona Olympic Gold medallist. Is she your sister?

"I love playing badminton, you know. During my High School years, I won several trophies."

"I wish she were my sister. She is a Chinese Indonesian like me. No, we were not related. Susanti is not even a family name. It's a meaningless word. Susanto is a common Indonesian surname. I had to change my birth name Thia-eng Ong to Grace Susanti when I turned eighteen, otherwise it would be extremely hard to enroll in the State universities and to apply for a passport or to obtain an ID card with an alien Chinese-sounding name. Even Susi, after all the glory she contributed to her motherland, had to produce the Certificate Proof of Citizenship to renew her passport."

"Why should you discard your Chinese birth name? Was it mandatory?"

"No, it was not. However as a law-abiding citizen, one had to follow all regulations without questioning the practicality or the motive behind them. After the failed attempt by the PKI-Indonesian Communist Party on 30 September 1965 to grab power from the ailing President Soekarno, the Soeharto regime severed ties with China, which was allegedly supporting PKI. One million PKI sympathizers were eradicated, including tens of thousands of Chinese Indonesians. "Three millions," bragged—accompanied with a smug smile—the fearsome Red Beret RPKAD Commander General Sarwho Eddie. He spoke, as if Communist souls were worthless as bed bugs. Indonesia was engulfed in the killing frenzy of communists spearheaded by the Muslim youth organizations, backed and blessed by the military.

Then followed the discriminative 1967 Change Name Act created by General Soemitro who prided himself in his memoir "From Mulawarman Territorial Commander to the Supreme Commander of Security and Order," that he was the mastermind behind the banning of all Chinese related culture, be it Chinese books, newspaper, speaking Chinese in public, Chinese New Year celebration and all festivities. Wow! What a heroic achievement of a patriotic soldier. The Act strongly recommended all Indonesians of Chinese descent to change their names and adopt names friendly and acceptable to Indonesian ears. They believed that Indonesian-sounding names would accelerate the integration of this "exclusive" minority. In hindsight, General Soemitro was to be applauded for his "creativity." Had he studied the Holocaust in earnest, he would have introduced a more drastic measure! Like Jews in the concentration camps, no name allowed but only numbers!

Fiona sighed, with a tinge of empathy in her voice to the plight of this vulnerable ethnic minority: "They must be a bunch of paranoids."

•

Back to my window seat after an hour-long conversation with Fiona pouring out all my grievances, I peeped through the shade-drawn oval window. It was pitch dark. Strangely enough, I felt how happy I was, when the plane finally prepared for landing at the Perth International Airport.

Hearing the screeching of airplane tires rubbing the hard bitumen and feeling a sudden jolt caused by the jets' reverse thrust, I wiped my tears, when I remembered the words of the late Martin Luther King Jr., shortly before he was gunned down by the white supremacist Earl Spencer Ray in April 1968 in Memphis:

"The greatest tragedy is not the brutality by the evil people, but rather the silence of good people."

Until today not a single perpetrator, let alone the mastermind of the May 1998 Rape of Jakarta has been brought to justice. Nobody seemed to care any longer. The raped victims were "only" Chinese Indonesian girls and woman. I had to live with my disabled body. Without my Fallopian tubes, do I have the right to be considered a woman?

●

Happiness No.1: To start a new life in a strange new country which out of compassionate reason had given me, one of the organized gang rape victims during the May 1998 Rape of Jakarta, a refuge. How I treasure the three-year renewable protection visa! I had crossed the Rubicon. My sorrow was squashed by an ineffable joy.

Grace Susanti's life has been full of sorrows. Born in Jakarta in 1972 as the youngest daughter of a small grocery shop owner, she is a Chinese Indonesian minority, female, and Roman Catholic. She failed to get her medical degree after what happened on that fateful afternoon, May 14, 1998. Currently she lives in Western Australia with her dog, Milo, a Labrador and Otis, her Siamese cat. She works as a nurse in a hostel for elderly people.

How Prostate Cancer Made a Man of Me
Hal Ackerman

"HOW I FOUND OUT"

I always thought it would be my heart. My father's conked out on him before he was fifty. My uncle's and grandfather's too. I do all the right things to counter my genetics; no red meat or tobacco, an approximation of tennis three times a week, an annual physical. All the paper umbrellas we hold up against the thousand pound safe that's falling at us from an indeterminate distance. Dr. Gilbert Norton is the head of Family Health at the University Medical Center where I teach. He makes small talk about our respective students as he thumps and listens and probes and prods. I come this close to escaping without any bad news. I have gotten dressed. We have made the parting pleasantries. I have one foot out the door when he asks as a casual afterthought, "Have we checked your PSA lately?" The question carries with it the burden of responsible upkeep. (When was the last time we checked that transmission fluid, those fan belts?) I mumble that I think it's been a year. He says it's been two and suggests that we ought to do a digital exam. Lest there be any misunderstanding surrounding the phrase digital examination, it is not an examination of the digits. It is an examination by the digits into an area beyond the digits' easy reach.

"I feel a roughness on one side," he says. I feel the expression in his voice change. The color of the room changes. My breathing changes. "Was this ever here before?" Why the hell is he asking me? It's his goddamn job to know. But of course he knows. And of course I know. It was not there before. He tells me not to get too concerned until we see the results of the PSA test. He draws a vial of blood.

At this moment my ignorance of my own body is monumental. I have never heard of the term Prostate Specific Androgen. And for the prostate gland itself? It's like Bulgaria. No one is quite sure where it is or what goes on there. When he calls me the following day there is no small talk about students. My PSA has come back at 11.8. I have no standard to measure that by but I hear no sigh of relief in his voice. I ask him what's normal for someone my age. I'm ready to hear seven or eight. I brace myself for six. "Around two or three," he says. "Anything over four we get a little concerned." Before I can stop myself, I blurt out a question that contains the words "I" and "cancer" in closer proximity than I have ever spoken those two words before. He gives me the name of a urologist who will perform a biopsy.

"BIOPSY"

Doctor Fish's nurse/receptionist is a woman with tight curled hair and a sheaf of papers on a clipboard. Not many men come away from here with good news, but experience has softened her the way a river changes limestone. She brings me into a small and sterile cubicle populated with the tools of the urology trade— rubber gloves, K-Y jelly. She notes the answer to my questions on a chart. Difficulty in starting urination? Dribbling after urination? Discomfort with urination? Dark urine? Blood in urine? Inability to hold urine? Inability to get erection?

I don't mind the questions. I've been in the LA single scene for so long, the interrogation sounds like a first date. Dr. Fish is a man in his fifties who must have squeezed 10,000 prostate glands in his career. Some small and healthy and juicy as a kiwi, some swollen to the size of a cantaloupe, some hard and nodulery as a handful of marbles. I assume the position and brace myself. A needle at the end of a miniature slingshot is shot five centimeters into the gland and retrieves tissue sample. Think about jabbing a hot dog on the grill to see if it's ready. This is done twelve times. It does not become easier with repetition. I spend the next two days not thinking about it at all. If I ignore it, it can't hurt me. I realize this is my mother's strategy about bees. Which doesn't even work on bees.

"You've got a good bit of cancer there," are the words he uses when he brings me the results of the biopsy. "Cancer in nine of the twelve cores. He assures me that if I had to get cancer, this was the best kind to get. His inflection, the philosophical nod of the head, are so well practiced that they seem spontaneously derived for this performance. I wait confidently for his nurse to burst into the office brandishing a fax from the testing lab "Dear Mister Ackerman, Boy are our faces red. We sent the results to the wrong guy. It is he, not you that must face his own mortality. We regret the inconvenience and hope you'll think of us for all your future cancer-screening needs." When I return to reality he is discussing the efficacy of surgery. I can barely grasp the cognates: catheters, incontinence, impotence. Three-to-six-months recovery. And that's if everything goes right. You're cutting past a lot of delicate apparatus here. One slip and you're singing soprano... (Oh, sorry. Did you want those?) But beyond that, after even a successful surgery, after the ripping open the tearing out, after the healing the putting back together; if one single cancer cell has slipped away unnoticed, migrated out of the capsule, made it to the blood stream, made a tiny settlement in a bone, then that whole ordeal will have been for nothing. Radiation would then be necessary or chemo.

Johnny, tell the audience and the contestants what's behind door number TWO. Behind Door #2 is—RAY-DEE-A-SHUN. Yes, radiation. Spend fifty-six glorious days getting NUKED. Be your own personal Ground Zero. Enjoy radiation colitis, the fierce and sudden desire to pee and the inability to do so. And! That's just the UP side. Like with surgery, if any cells escape the bombardment. It's chemo, baby, chemo.

I want to hear, "Wake up" and this never happened. But the first thing cancer takes away are all the easy choices. He has already set up a consultation with the radiation oncologist who will be doing my MRI and bone scan. My mind is on a ten-second tape delay. It takes that long for it to register that he means that I am to have a MRI and bone scan to see whether the cancer has metastasized. My cancer. That I am to have it now. I take the elevator down three levels into sub-sub-basement. There are yellow signs pointing toward Nuclear Medicine. My natural instinct would be to flee such signs. I never even use a microwave. Yet I follow. I feel ridiculously obedient. Sick and dire people wearing hospital gowns and painful expressions walk dazedly through the corridor. I don't belong here. I feel too healthy. I have never experienced one single symptom of the disease. I am strapped down into a body tray and cautioned not to move or breathe while a probe is inserted into my rectum and inflated to the size of a squirrel. Autonomous mechanisms whir and groan underneath me and a featureless cocoon slowly covers my body, first to my chest, then to my chin until I am completely enclosed in a shell half an inch from my face.

To avoid claustrophobia I close my eyes and visualize endless galaxies, a universe of stars falling all around me like a snow dome. After twenty minutes the probe is deflated and removed and I am brought next door for the bone scan. I catch fragments of conversation between the technicians as they read the preliminary results. One of them uses the term "hot spots." The other says they better take some more pictures.

It is 5:30 in the afternoon when I return to the outside world. The sky has an exceptional fall glow, cobalt blue with streaks of reddish orange clouds, and I have cancer. There is an exciting hint of a bite in the air and I have cancer. People are walking across the long promenade coming in and out of the building. Their kids run before them, erratic and thoughtless. And I have cancer. I drive homewardly and try to keep the future inflated in front of me but I can't erase the mental images of that second group of X-rays dotted with pulsating points of light. Hot spots. Galaxies of disease. I put a Tom Waits song on that has a repeating refrain, "Hold on, hold on, babe you got to hold on." I hold on. My daughter has just turned twenty; the age I was when my own father died. The weight of all the things I have not taught her yet falls on my head like a closet full of bowling pins. I plan the music for my funeral.

It is nearly dark when I get home. There's a current of fresh smelling air as day turns to night. I remember walking down Ocean Parkway in Brooklyn on fall evenings when I was a child, carrying home a loaf of rye bread still warm from the bakery. The streets were filled with men coming home from work, carrying brief cases and adult concerns. I want to be a child among them now, comfortably invisible; my hands tucked into my pockets, a loaf of warm bread nestled under my jacket, cool fresh air with the smell of burning leaves in my nose, knowing that when I get home there will be a hot bowl of soup waiting for me. Dr. Fish's nurse/receptionist calls the next day. The test results are clear. The hotspots were pockets of arthritis from old sports injuries. There is no spread. I let her words roll down over my head like hot fudge over ice cream. I feel so lucky to merely have prostate cancer.

"CHEMICAL EUNUCH"

It was my oldest friend's older brother who led me to Hormone Deprivation Therapy. It works against cancer the way cancer works against a healthy body. It starves it of its food supply. It creates the ultimate embargo. Unfortunately, its food supply is testosterone; the very hormone that defines our maleness. To prostate cancer cells testosterone is nature's most perfect food. It is like spinach to Popeye. Like mother's milk. And in the Garden of Eden into which they are placed, their entire environment is edible. Imagine living in a city made of chocolate. Within six months, a man's hormonal chemistry most closely resembles that of women in menopause. We experience hot flashes. Night sweats. Muscle tone evaporates. Fat accumulates around the middle. The threat of osteoporosis increases. Some men experience breast enlargement. (If that happens to me, two friends of mine want to date me.)

In the twelve months I was on the medication my PSA shrunk down to 0.02. But not without a price. The normal level of male testosterone is 500-600. At the end of a year, mine was 10. Libido? Gone. Not only is the sex drive gone, but the desire for the sex drive is gone. Women, whose bodies in the past would have stimulated longing and desire, now generate no more response than the sight of uncovered furniture. Unaided spontaneous erectility is a distant memory. That Saturday Night Special, decays into Flaccido Domingo. There is something strangely liberating about being immune to physical stimuli. It's like seeing a puppet show from backstage. You see how all the tricks are done, but the magic is gone. The other downside is that hormone deprivation does not kill the cancer. For that, a *coup de grace* is needed, the implantation of radioactive seeds. For this, I have decided to go to Seattle, home base of Dr. John Blasco, who has pioneered this procedure called Brachytherapy.

"THE COUP DE GRACE"

It is a year since Dr. Norton found that "rough spot." Flying into Seattle, I see a mantle of snow off the crest of Mt. Rainier. Traffic from the airport is light. My driver has a long black beard and a blue turban and speaks in that lovely cadence of the subcontinent. He finds my hotel easily. I am buzzed through the outside glass door into the musty vestibule. Streaks of weakened sunlight struggle in through layers of window soot and velour curtains. The smell of something cooked in the 1940s permeates the velvet nub of purple carpet. The man checking in before me wheels an oxygen tank alongside him on a shopping cart. He is frail and blotched. He looks like a stunted tree with patches of fungus on its bark. I keep myself at a distance, not wanting to breathe the same air. I am not like him. I am healthy. His wife fusses over the arrangements. She moves with difficulty and seems cross with everything around her. I wonder what binds this couple. It can't just be their shared maladies. They could not have expected to end up this way. Yet there is a strange testy affection between them, even if they have to repeat everything four times. Maybe that's the secret. Less communication. I don't know why I didn't let my new girlfriend, Patty, come with me. She wanted to. I find strange solace in the anonymity. In my last dream before waking I am strapped to a log on the St. Lawrence River, and a huge buzz saws was cutting off slices of my leg. Tough one to interpret. At 6:00 a.m. I follow the directions on the little green fleet enema box. I will spare you the details except to say that if all consumer products were equally effective we'd be a happy nation.

I walk to the hospital in the bleak and warming early morning sunlight. I take the elevator to the Seattle Prostate Clinic. I'm greeted cheerfully by the nurse, who calls me by my first name though we have never met. She asks cheerfully whether I've had my enema, and I answer cheerfully that I have. We're all so cheerful. I am given a gown to change into and told to empty my bladder. In the restrooms of the prostate center all the toilet seats are up. And suddenly the eighteen-month waiting is over. I am not just going to Seattle as I had blithely referred to it. I am receiving final treatment for cancer. I walk under my own power across an interior ramp to the operating theater. I meet the anesthesiologist. He administers a spinal and I am numbed from the waist down. I am wheeled into the operating room. My feet are placed in stirrups and a long thin needle is inserted. I close my eyes and listen to the sounds of the procedure going on all around me. The seeds are placed into the needle. The computerized map leads Blasco's sure hand. He has done this four thousand times. This is my first and only. I encircle myself with images of people who love me; old dear friends and family. My students. Annie, my daughter. My mother is not there. I have not told her about any of this. It is not out of altruism. I cannot bear the weight of her concern.

A couple of hours later I'm walking out under my own power. I take a taxi back to the hotel. The feeling has come back to my legs. My tush feels like I've given birth rectally to a porcupine, but that eases up as the day progresses. Twenty-four hours after I arrived, I get back on the plane to Los Angeles. I wonder, when all this is over, when radioactive seeds have killed the cancer and I'm off the hormones, and my testosterone returns to normal levels, whether I will become again the man I was, or are we all merely products of our chemistry. What makes a man a man? As Mt. Rainier retracts into the distance, I recall the day when I told my daughter that I had been diagnosed with cancer. Tears shot from her eyes like they had fifteen years earlier when her mother and I told her we were getting divorced. She had not sat in my lap for years, but she ran across the room to me and threw her arms around me and cried. I made her look at me and told her that it was going to be all right; that I had waited until I knew that it was going to be all right so that when I told her she would know that it was true. A mother has a child's love whatever she does. A father has to earn every small moment of it, by explaining and making safe for his child a world that still frightens him and that he's never understood.

The landing gear shudders into place and I am jostled into half-wakefulness. The plane settles down into the familiar hazy blanket of smog and headlights. Traffic is light on the way home. There are lights on in the house when I get home. Annie has waited up for me. She has made me hot soup.

Hal Ackerman is co-area head of the UCLA Screenwriting program. His fiction and poetry have appeared in numerous literary journals, most recently in The Pinch, The Southeast Review, *and the anthology,* I Wanna Be Sedated. *His one-man play,* Testosterone, *based upon the events in this essay, premiered in 2007.*

Trauma Chic
Holly Leigh

Today I am a starfish. My body, tuned by instinct and memory, stretches in all directions. When I exercise, I am reaching for things beyond my grasp.

"Arabesque," calls the aerobic instructor who wields us like pinwheels with her commands. Hamstring, biceps, quads, each part named in turn. From my place, I study all the contours of a chorus line of women stretched, legs apart, arms extended in an open V.

"Abductor," calls Jessica. We imitate star shapes, and I mimic the muscled limbs, unblemished and whole, of the promising pony-tailed university women, replicas of my former self.

A car-fire severely scarred my face and ruined my hands when I was twenty-three. Now I live the "hand" in handicapped, moving through the architecture of the everyday world. Coins defy my awkward grasp. I gripe about smooth industrial-style doorknobs or those sticky with antiquity, about layers of packaging. I avoid buttons, belts, zippers; even snaps on clothing can trap me. At the gym, I must ask someone each time to tie my sneakers' shoelaces. But I find it's the obstacle of people's attitude and perceptions that most often trips me.

Before class started, a woman in neon spandex made a beeline through the Cybex machines until she reached me.

"I've seen you," she said and everyone looked up.

"I must tell you, you are so brave, really, and a real inspiration—I just want you to know that." I said nothing, hoping to embarrass her with my implacable stare. But she bounced off oblivious.

Strangers know nothing about me, yet I find I've been assigned a new persona based solely on my changed look. Fending off "sensitive" remarks is the most tedious part of my day.

"I think I have problems, then I see you," is one winner. "Brave" and "courageous" are labels that create caricatures of disability.

"I don't know how you do it, I could never, I can't imagine," others say and behind the gush of praise lurks a shady superiority. A line of separation exists:

I am marked as different, isolated, out on some nether planet.

I stroll past all the bodies squeezing or rowing or treading on machines. We all are stripped down here, almost bare. In this cocoon of a sweat lodge, I hope women come for strength, power, satisfaction in the physical realm. But as on the outside, every greeting is about weight, clothes, hair, looks. Anyone disfigured is alien or suspect. But no makeup or prosthetic device can fix my looks.

"Once you've had surgery, you'll be fine," people rush to say, not realizing I've had over 80 operations. Many people feel the need to approach and commend me or comment on the latest medical breakthrough they've just seen on 20/20. People freely tell me their intimate medical details, trace out faded scars, describe their dream nose job or dispense random advice. They inform me of people with prosthetic limbs playing pianos or the wonders of artificial skin. At the gym, I hear, "Hi, I'm a nurse," which invokes the patient role as my identity outside the hospital. Addressing the damage first cancels me as a person. Every mention stuns me, each sharp reminder feels like running into barbed wire.

"You're lucky, you're so skinny," is the code compliment everyone gives me. But being so thin that your hips hurt when you lie on one side or so bony in the bathtub that you feel every vertebra is not fun. After years of hospitals and months of being confined during surgery, I have trouble opposite the norm. Working out is my sole key to appetite, sleep, thinking. When I skip the gym, my weight drops, so I like the small swell of muscle, calves and a thigh that fits snug in my pant leg. But I suffer from a symmetry complex. One leg scarred from hip to ankle, one arm gone, one breast marred, one eye ruined.

I really never know how or what to expect from people on the street. Once, a guy standing beside me at a crosswalk told me I looked like a living incarnation of a damaged goddess statue. "Oh," was my meager surprised answer. Later, I appreciated his creative candor. I wondered if he was a sculptor, art student or teacher.

"You have trauma chic," a friend tells me. He's coined a term for the trail of turned heads I leave in my wake when I go grocery shopping, browse at bookstores, hop on the subway or walk into a restaurant. I have x-ray vision. Twelve years of fielding public inquiry has developed an acute awareness. My face holds a mirror to yours. Your reaction, whether invasive, respectful or indifferent speaks volumes about you.

Trauma perks do exist. My usually invisible status turns into celebrity stature on airlines. Being bumped up to first class or hustled through passport lines adds to the trauma chic aura. I don't say no to pity, concert tickets or free coffees. Last week, I had three women at a florist shop doting on me as they pulled together the lavish flowers and ribbons I needed for a gift. Some gestures tip the balance back or simply surprise me.

Once, right after surgery, my friend, Mona, convinced me to go out to a fancy restaurant even though I had a circle of gauze wrapped elaborately around my head. Fresh red patches of blood showed underneath, and though the restaurant was darkly lit, I knew people were staring. Undeterred, we lingered over coffee and desserts and when the waiter told us an anonymous patron had picked up our expensive dinner tab, Mona was amazed.

"So there are good people in the world," she laughed. She suggested I dress in bandages from now on.

By the gym lockers, a polite woman glances over as I brace the key against my arm. Without fingers, I can still manage to turn and open these flimsy locker doors as well as I work my apartment locks at home.

"I never know when to offer help," she says. I nod, liking her casual tone. I tell her it's nice if someone asks if I need anything but not out of the blue or as an excuse to delve into medical topics. Skip any inspirational comments, I think. Trauma savvy means treating difference without undue familiarity or judgment and definitely without ceremony.

In class, I stand far back from the mirrored walls in the aerobic classes. No face, just a body in motion. We get close to swimming with the liquid sweat, fluid selves moving in our spandex skins as if bathing in underwater currents. We are closed in by an aquarium-like glass wall, as the music flows in a rhythmic stream.

"Relevé," calls Heidi, our ballet boot camp leader. We stretch on tiptoes.

"Glissade," she calls, and like dancing stars, we leap from one foot to the other. Another step sequence and our legs are cutting the air in diamond shapes. For the allotted hour, an audible pulse threads through our inner ligaments, tendons, quads, flexed toes like a wave, moving us through the choreographed sequences. During this time, I breathe deeply, feeling both joined and anonymous, a part of the flow.

Afterward, as I stretch, splayed out across the wood floor, I think of the starfish as a motif. A hand with the strength of a fist, enough to open a clam and the power to regenerate an arm. Today I wish to be a starfish. Gliding effortlessly through my day, my life. Unnoticed. Healed.

Holly Leigh has published poems and essays in The Alembic, Bardsong, Bellevue Literary Review, Christian Science Monitor, Colorado Review, Fugue, The Healing Muse, New England Writers Anthology, Pilgrimage, Practical Horseman, *and* Redwood Coast Review. *She has since given up the gym to ride and jump horses, a former passion.*

Trying on New Glasses
Diana Lund

"The logic is kindergarten," I'd started my therapy session. From the cues of the week's events written on a red 3x5 card, I reconstructed the milk debacle. "Each day I discover something out of place, like a gallon of milk on the kitchen counter. When I touch the container, it feels warm and I know then that it has sat out for an hour or more. But thinking back over the day, I have no recollection of drinking milk. I want to accuse my roommate of being the culprit because I certainly didn't sour the milk. Yet, I live alone. Logically, the only person I can accuse is me."

"But Diana," the psychologist said, smiling with the beam of a light bulb moment, "you can fault that other person living inside of you, the one that the brain injury brings out. Let's call her Marcia."

With the smack of a hammer splitting a rock, Shazam! Marcia was born.

I considered her my evil twin. Marcia left the doors to my car and house unlocked and sometimes open. Other times she locked me out of the house for hours in the cold, under dressed, until my boyfriend or a neighbor with a spare key or a policeman with a crowbar arrived. Marcia left the indoor cats outside all night. Marcia hid my things, including my car, in the most unusual of places. She heated the oven all night long, burnt most of my meals, and started kitchen fires that turned my pans to charcoal. Marcia left tasks half-completed as if she had been kidnapped in the middle of a job. I'd walk into these scenes—a dryer door open with wet clothes inside or half of the laundry folded—incredulous at her lack of concentration or her distractibility. Marcia was hard to live with. I could get angry at Marcia. I could laugh at Marcia.

As I got to know Marcia and her antics, I saw a need to take back some control from her. No pills and no treatments exist to combat evil twins. Instead, about all a doctor could do in 1996 to help a patient cope with a brain injury that directs the show was teach compensatory strategies the tools of adaptation.

Each compensatory strategy needs to be matched to the level of the injury as education is matched to age. If the brain is not ready or needs rest, it will not learn. Give the injured brain too many tactics when we cannot parallel process and we overload, rendering the ideas useless. Tell the injured brain to rest for an hour at two each day when we have lost the concept of time, and we miss some of the rest we need. A compensatory strategy is only as good as its probable execution.

With my therapist, we developed a game plan. (Others with better medical insurance might undergo rehabilitation.) She was the brain of the operation.

"Diana, my biggest concern for you at home is those regular kitchen fires. We need to put measures in place so that they don't happen again."

"Uh-huh."

"Now, one kitchen fire scenario goes like this. You start rice on the stove, leave the kitchen, and then forget that you are cooking."

"Yeah, I do that a lot."

"What you need is a reminder that you are cooking."

"Okay."

"Do you own a microwave?"

"Yes, I do."

"Before you leave the kitchen, I want you to set the timer on the microwave to alert you when the rice is done cooking."

"Uh, I don't cook rice in the microwave. I cook it on the stove."

"No, no. I don't want you to cook the rice in the microwave, I only want you to use the timer on the microwave."

"Uh, don't I have to cook something in the microwave to use the timer?"

"No, you don't. It has a timer function. Okay, let's scratch that plan. Do you have a kitchen timer?"

"Huh? What? What is a kitchen timer?"

By the end of the session I had written down: Set timer to indicate when food is done.

At home, I examined my microwave and still technologically savvy, figured out how to use the timer. Remembering to set the timer, however, was my impediment. I had to burn meals to remind myself of my frustration with cooking, which might or might not have led to recalling my timer solution. I might have needed to see the note from my therapy session, and then, immediately, to create a large sign: USE TIMER FOR COOKING, and then to place my sign in an obvious location next to the stove. When cooking, I might not have seen that sign and then forgotten to set the timer again. After a month or two, I might have turned using a timer into a habit. Yet, after I had established the habit and taken down the sign, I still might have forgotten to use the timer and consequently burned my food.

Say I remembered to set the timer. As soon as I left the kitchen, I forgot about the timer and my cooking. Sometime later, perhaps while I sat in my living room, I'd hear the timer ring and ask myself, What was that noise in the kitchen? Curious, I stumbled to the kitchen and magically, like I was rich and had a professional cook on my staff, I found a hot meal on the stove with pan unscathed. Learning new habits was hit or miss, a smidgen of luck, and an operable brain day.

When my boyfriend Rick saw the timer sign in my kitchen, he jumped into the act and helped me to develop more cues. Tackling his biggest worries for me, my unlocked/open doors and my erratic driving (sometimes I drove okay and other times not), he suggested signs: Are the doors locked? and Am I conscious enough to drive? I copied his words on Post-it notes and stuck one at eye-level along the stairway to my bedroom and the other on the steering wheel of my car. I could never tell if I was conscious enough to drive. As it was, I always answered Yes to that question. In retrospect, a better set of questions would have been: Did you get a good night's sleep? Have you spent most of the day in a quiet, dark environment? If not, have you done any brain-intensive activities today? If so, has your brain had enough rest?

A few weeks later my therapist suggested, "Write down what you want to remember in a journal. Then you can reference it to fill in the blanks you will have later on." In the same session, she added, "The act of writing increases the chance that you will remember what you wrote about. So, you may not even need to reference an event in your journal because, instead, you have remembered it." After this discussion, we referred to my journal as my memory book.

Months later, I came up with another motive to write in my journal: the unpredictability of my life's course was fascinating. My former life had been foreseeable. Study hard. Get a degree. Find a good job. Buy a house. Nowhere in the plan did I read: Get in a car accident. Become whimsical. Unravel.

●

At my home and office, visitors noticed how slovenly I'd become. Stacks of papers littered tables and desks. Numerous Post-it notes, Don't forget your keys or Buy milk at the grocery store, were affixed to vertical surfaces. On the floor sat several items in the middle of a path, forcing one to step over them to pass. At entrances lay a line-up of goods—borrowed possessions, dirty clothes for dry cleaning, my leather briefcase—which made it impossible to open or close a door without moving the obstacles first. My surroundings, an eyesore, contrasted my old image—the neatnik. Uninformed observers concluded that I'd slipped down a muddy hill and into the pits of squalor.

They didn't recognize that I'd expended great effort to arrange my environment this way; the disorder possessed an order. The top layer of papers corresponded to tasks needing immediate completion. The Post-its, scraps of my brain, reminded me to do things I otherwise would have forgotten. The laundry basket in the middle of my living room floor dislodged the memory that I was washing clothes. And the location of my briefcase forced me to pick up the case before I could leave the house or the office. The messes represented a positive sign that I was learning compensatory strategies.

Besides systematizing my physical environment, the other key to reducing my stress was a detailed well-balanced schedule. With my therapist's help, I reorganized. I moved from a week-at-a-glance datebook to a month-at-a-glance calendar to widen my vista. In the monthly view I combined my work activities with my social activities with my to-do list with my phone book, previously kept separately, and retained my memory bank within arm's reach as best I could.

Each Sunday Rick worked with me to schedule the next week's activities, coordinating his schedule with mine. Around my seventh-month mark a dab of planning capability returned, which gave Rick something to work with during our lengthy scheduling sessions.

To create my schedule, I rated activities on a scale of one to ten based on their brain intensiveness. On the low end of the scale sat physical therapy and massage sessions. More stressful activities, fives, included walking to a small grocery store to shop or to the bank to get cash. Social activities with several people talking at once rated a ten, as did working at the corporate office, as did driving.

Even with all this scheduling, my life whirled out of control. I was impulsive, lost track of time, would forget to look at the schedule, and frequently got sick. Unforeseen things happened, such as having to spend an extra hour to retrieve a purse I'd left in an ice cream parlor. Some days I woke up too exhausted to follow the schedule. All of these circumstances impacted my adherence to the schedule and forced revision. Off-kilter, I scratched off social events first, then driving into work and meetings in person, and then work itself. Resting, physical therapy exercises, and doctor's visits became my top priorities. The on-the-run person, me, turned into a recluse.

Spontaneity died. I couldn't say impromptu, "Let's shop for groceries," because the sky might have been dark (night blindness prevented me from driving at night), or I had driven my allotment for that day, or the next day's schedule was a killer. Even if I ignored or forgot my rules and drove to the store with a list, I might not have functioned well enough to shop for the groceries, pay and drive home. I risked finding out in the middle of the activity, like driving, that my brain couldn't handle the event. When I sank fast, I thwarted the activity, at times abruptly, and quickly got myself to a safe place. I didn't want to harm myself or others. Sometimes I ran from embarrassment over what my sorry dysfunctional brain had done, over knocking over a cereal display in Jewel.

For the longest time, I thought that I could tell the state of my mind by how I felt. But crazy people can't tell from the inside how crazy they are. After a year, I understood that the internal measure on my steering wheel—Am I conscious enough to drive?—was ineffective. The only way I could gauge my brain's ineptness was to watch what happened when I tried to do something. Like a pilot checks out the plane's equipment, I learned to test myself for failure. Walk okay? Check. Read okay? Check. Play card game Solitaire okay? Check. Dissimilar to a captain's assessment, a check meant no more failure than usual.

Many times I didn't test out okay. After an excessively stimulating activity, like a wedding, my schedule's full day or two of rest was not enough of a down period—even if I instituted the no TV/music rule and spent my time sitting in silence or walking. With no other viable strategy, I waited and hoped that sometime soon my brain would refresh like a computer screen degausses.

Several months into the brain injury, a solution floated in to one of my biggest problems—following a schedule. When all the managers at work got Palm Pilots, I saw what the electronic scheduler could do and immediately bought one. Like a mother reminding her daughter, it beeped me fifteen minutes before a meeting and flashed the message, PREPARE FOR GROUP MEETING on its screen. Five minutes before the meeting's scheduled start, another beep sounded, prompting me to leave my cubicle. For physical therapy and psychotherapy, the Palm prodded me, and also when my wash was ready to be taken out of the dryer. With my personal prompter, I could follow a schedule as long as I did not misplace the Life Pilot or let the batteries run low.

About a year and a half after the accident, my whiplash pain, which lessened at a glacial pace, started to break up. With a little more energy, I decided to add yoga to my schedule, an excellent strategy.

The first year of class was like unsticking a body after a vat of rubber glue had been poured over it. The rubber kept pulling at my arms, legs and back in opposition to the way I was supposed to bend. Not only couldn't I perform the moves, but also I had trouble aligning my body in the correct position at the right time and coordinating my breathing to the sequence. During the Triangle, Fencer and Thread the Needle movements, commonly a classmate guided my hand or pointed to an out-of-place foot, hip or elbow.

In class, I always felt glad when we got to the last ten minutes: relaxation. As we rested on our mats, the teacher spoke softly, "Quieting the mind is hard to do. We all live busy lives and fill our minds all day long. Now is the time to relax. So, clear your mind. Don't think of anything. But if you have difficulty, like we all do, then think of white."

I had been one of those people. Silence was a gap requiring fill and I had trained my mind marvelously. When I was growing up, my parents didn't get along and would go long periods of time in angry silence with one another. Anxious in their joint presence, I'd either talked to one parent at a time or else brought my mind to other topics—to homework problems or a girlfriend's upcoming birthday party, anything but to a fight that would never resolve. Staying with the silence had seemed a deadly option.

Constant head chatter carried into adulthood, during work, driving, relaxing. I'd had problems to solve, events to plan, memories to replay. Each week I'd meditated to break from the parade, but soon into the trance, my mind would stop chanting or blanking out, and instead, would maneuver back to a stream of side thoughts. Playing sports, another tactic, had slowed, but had not squelched the shooting ideas. Inner silence, my lofty goal, only had entered my awake-life for seconds at a time, with a single exception. Once while in college, I'd paid to float in a dark, enclosed tank—naked. After I'd entered the small pool and lain supinely in the water, my mind had sped from idea to idea, until, drifting in the blackness for several minutes, my thoughts quelled. Because the temperature of the salty water matched my own, soon, I couldn't sense my body. In my disorientation, I also couldn't tell where the outside world ended and where I began. Terrifyingly, I'd lost my "self," while at the same time, inconceivable in a logical sense, "I" became one with a powerful silence of greater breadth than a galaxy. More mute inside my head than not, I'd hung in cosmos-limbo, about forty-five minutes, until the attendant startled me back to reality by banging on the tank. For the next two months, from one brush of an angel, I'd carried peace deep inside of me, the same peace I'd sensed once before emanating from a Hawaiian surfing instructor I'd met while on vacation.

Like hovering in a flotation temple, brain injury connected me to an absence of words which mysteriously washed a sereneness over me. So when the yoga teacher calmly whispered to still our minds, I thought, I have no trouble thinking of nothing. My trouble is thinking of something. Easily, I blanked my mind each session; nun-like, Zen-like, tranquil described my now, natural state. As if making up for years of head noise, my new genius (everyone is a genius at something) became silence of thought and in-the-moment living.

Great at relaxation, but awkward in movement, sooner or later, my self-consciousness in the exercise portion of the class was outweighed by the friendly classmates, the knowledgeable teacher, Janet, who gave me the individual attention I needed, and yoga's benefits: pain alleviation, health restoration, freer movement and a peaceful inner center.

After your memory improves to the point where you can remember that you have a bad memory and you understand what behaviors occur because of this, the dynamic changes. Take the discovery of milk on the counter. I no longer asked, "How did this happen?" I knew that I had left the milk out even though I had no recollection of doing so. Without hesitation, I dumped the milk down the sink and in the process realized that the milk was cold. I did not leave it out for hours, only minutes, and could have kept it. Recognition of my problem was progress, a progress that cultivated my yearning for recovery. Whatever recovery looked like, I had a feeling I would always need compensatory strategies.

Diana Lund is the author of memoir, Remind Me Why I'm Here: Sifting through Sudden Loss of Memory and Judgment, *about her life after a car accident. Lund has appeared on Chicago Public Radio and speaks at other venues in the Chicago area. Currently, she is writing a second book.*

The Space Left Behind After Loss
Robert Bradford Walker

SOUND ASLEEP

I was one of the fortunate ones, born into a culture that gave considerable deference toward those who had wealth, attractiveness, intelligence or status. As the son of a well-educated physician and an attractive socialite from Boston, I stepped into the familiar footprints that had been modeled by my parents and was swept unconsciously through childhood, prep school, college and military service. When it was time to step out into the world of my own choices, I took my first real job at a large community hospital, married a vibrant woman, had two energetic children, and settled into a comfortable home in an affluent suburb of Connecticut.

Each workday I would ease my vintage Porsche out of the garage, negotiate the steep, curved driveway, and glide gracefully through the Connecticut hillsides towards the inner city of Hartford. Once there, I would secrete my car in the far corner of the lot, step across the street towards the main entrance of the hospital and pat the life-size statue of a black Labrador dog ceremoniously on the head as I passed by. But now I was straining just to get a glimpse of it out the window of the Continuing Care Unit. It had only been two weeks since the minor car accident, which left me more concerned with the dent in my car than the fact I never saw the woman bolting through the intersection. However, Dr. Shapiro's words were still resonating in my ears: "Your eyes are just fine; the problem is behind them; you have a brain tumor!"

It felt like a soft veil settling around me, drawing me away from reality and placing me gently into a safety net of denial. I heard myself mumble, "Oh good, I'm glad I'm friends with Ben; he should know exactly what to do." Ben was the Chief of Neurosurgery in a department I managed, and a good friend of my father. The question that I might need glasses had skirted quickly past concern and anxiety, bypassing fear and terror altogether and rested in the numbing realm of denial. As I headed back towards the administration building, people still acknowledged me in the hallway as if nothing had changed. I was still carefully disguised in my tailored gray, three-piece suit with color-coordinated, silk necktie, and black wing-tipped shoes that quietly announced my presence on the polished marble floors. But just as I rounded the corner to my office, I thought I heard a quiet voice whispering in my ear," this one is all mine; he is sound asleep!"

THE WAKE UP CALL

Hanging this tailored "uniform" in the narrow locker provided in each patient's room, I slipped into the denuding hospital "jonnie" that had been left for me on the corner of the bed. After a few futile attempts to tie the strings, I slipped under the starched sheets in hopes of preserving what little privacy I had left. The plastic covered pillow protested loudly as I settled back on the mattress, but it was too late. The waves of fear and vulnerability swept over me as I pulled the cold sheets as high as I could around my neck. So this was the view from the other side of the bed!

The surgery took almost fourteen hours. The small benign cyst that had been removed from my lung shortly after discharge from Vietnam had apparently metastasized to the occipital lobe of my brain. Ben tried to remove as much of the cancer as possible, but he had to take a considerable portion of my skull to reach the marauding cells that had already invaded the bone and extended down towards my brain stem. But this invasion was nothing compared to the headache that accompanied me to the recovery room. This surgery eventually became the beginning of the end of my life, and it started with an unusual challenge—to learn how to make friends with pain.

During my recovery, I began noticing that the footprints I had borrowed from my parents didn't fit very well with these challenges. The plethora of boarding schools and camps had nurtured some useful survival skills but the familiar sense of abandonment now included my body, my self, even God. I wasn't prepared for disability that had even removed my ability to see the statuesque Rover guarding the entrance to the hospital. My entire world had suddenly become gray and blurred as I tried to navigate my way around the rehabilitation unit. A few cracked shins and a terrifying slam to the side of my head sent me scurrying back to bed, clutching the call button as if it was my only lifeline to the outside world. I no longer felt responsible for changing my life; life had just changed me. In just a few weeks, this thirty-one-year-old hospital administrator had become a frightened, visually impaired, terminally ill cancer patient. The self-assured posture began to crack, break into pieces and eventually disappear into the enveloping abyss of fear.

MAKING SPACE

The losses came quickly after that, including my health, employment, house savings, marriage, children, even the beloved Porsche disappeared when radiation retinopathy nudged me towards a status of legal blindness. Two more craniotomies had left me permanently bald, boasting dents and scars that often invoke that fear-based curiosity towards those of us who are disabled, unattractive, unintelligent or poor. I had become invisible for the first time in my life, catching my first glimpse of what it might be like to die, before I had died

My heart had stopped twice during surgery but unfortunately, I wasn't rewarded with any dramatic out of body experiences or amazing white light drawing me towards the safety of some "larger room". I felt stuck on this earth plane, wondering what the hell had just happened to me. Then, in the spring of 1979, I finally heard the ominous words, "You have about six months to live". Still married at that time, I left my residency in Boston, packed my wife and two young children into the Volvo station wagon and headed west towards Tucson, Arizona. We had selected the desert because it was warm, had plenty of space and seemed like the perfect place to spend the remaining months of my life. The most recent brain surgery had been followed by extensive radiation; however both had failed to stem the rapid growth of the tumor.

Shortly after arriving in Tucson, I became so disorientated, my wife put the children in a crisis care center and took me to the emergency room of the local University Hospital. A young, courageous neurosurgeon evaluated my status and suggested something he cryptically called his "roto rooter procedure"—go for all the cancer he could find and see what I woke up with the next day! I didn't have many choices, so I agreed. Ben flew out from Connecticut to assist in this unusual procedure which resected more than one quarter of my brain, covered what was remaining with a cadaver's durra and installed shunts in hopes they might regulate the intracranial pressure.

I did wake up, and the procedure had been "successful", however I quickly retreated into a coma when my body began to reject the prosthesis that had replaced the back of my skull. A local dentist, who enjoyed sculpting as a hobby, had offered to take a mold of my head and fashion an implant out of the acrylic material used to make false teeth. This way my exposed brain would be protected, and perhaps a normal shaped head might relieve some of the constant stares that become familiar to persons with disabilities. So there I was, with a brand new head covering the same old façade, but it was so beaten and worn by this time, I began to die. Without noticing, I had quietly joined a community of the invisible and anonymous.

A few weeks later, a resident making his psychiatric rounds through the Intensive Care Unit, yanked me out of the safety of this "cocoon." He twisted my nipple so hard, I burst out of this peaceful place screaming at the top of my lungs, "You hurt me!" I was finally getting respite from the pain and some jackass decides I should come back for a little more? I was so angry; bellowing at the top of my lungs at anyone or anything in the room. Nurses and technicians scattered in all directions but none as fast as the young psychiatrist who had just become the focus of all my rage. I didn't mind dying; I even welcomed it after climbing into the safety of my cocoon. I could still hear the voices "out there" expressing concerns and solutions, but I felt safe," until that son-of-a-bitch wrenched my tit into purple! I was dancing peacefully with my last choice between life and death." And someone else makes the decision to yank me back! Why me?

The anger was so powerful I was unable to squeeze back into the safety of my cocoon. But once exhausted, I collapsed into an existence that I would hardly call living. I felt totally alone, and any trace of footprints I might have borrowed for a belief system, had morphed into unconscious habits and unusable blind spots. I felt like a man on automatic pilot, with only my fear, pain, blindness, and an overwhelming sense of aloneness to keep me company.

THE MIRACLE

In October of 1985, I woke-up totally confused and disoriented. I was lying on the bathroom floor of my small one-bedroom apartment, but when I reached up to sooth my crushing headache, the hair on the side of my head was caked with dried blood. I had little memory of what had happened the night before and slumping back onto the tiled floor, I could hear myself take in a long breath and then let it out very slowly, as if I was finally letting go. It was like the last bit of energy had drifted out of my body and "I didn't feel alive anymore" just barely surviving. Every breath felt like an entire lifetime, and I didn't even notice when another doctor, at another hospital told me, "it has to come out."

Apparently, somebody had unwrapped me from around the toilet and taken me to a medical center, where it was determined I had a grand mal seizure. The hospitalization, angiographies and subsequent surgery all seemed a blur, until I woke up in the recovery room. The surgeon was bending over me saying "I don't understand much of this, but I just removed a small benign tumor with some attached necrotic tissue that was located centerline in your brain. It appears this new cyst had cut off the blood supply that had been nourishing the inoperable cancer and post-operative x-rays indicate you are cancer-free!" From some distant place, I heard myself mumbling, "After six surgeries and all this preparation to die, you're telling me I'm going to live?" Strange as it might seem, I was profoundly disappointed.

THE HEALING

It was only a few weeks later when the huge jumbo-jet lifted off the runway and headed east towards London, the first leg on my journey to a remote, spiritual community on the northern coast of Scotland. I still had a large bandage wrapped around my head and upon landing at Heathrow Airport, was classified as a "harmless eccentric" before given directions to the overnight train for Inverness. I had been to Findhorn a few years earlier and was intrigued by the cooperative rhythm of this community, which had discovered a common spirituality in the impeccable honesty of nature. But most of all, I remembered feeling unusually safe during that workshop in this little village by the North Sea. But this time, I had my own agenda. I wanted to change before being changed again! I had learned about fear up close and personal, and understood it would always be about loss or being in lack, but I didn't know what rested in that space left behind afterwards? I was still blaming anybody or anything to help explain the unexplainable but I couldn't hear any answers, when I didn't even have the questions!

I arrived at the community, still posturing a few remnants of my battered self, but few seemed to notice. A few days later, tears began brimming from my wounded eyes as the pain of the past few years began to unravel. It wasn't long before I was sobbing uncontrollably in the Gardens at Calurn, where I had decided to work so I could be alone, while composting the waste from the community into the nourishment for the extensive fields and gardens. The more I interacted with the rhythm of nature and shared in the vision of the community, the more the tears began to lessen my fear and pain. Each morning I would attune with fellow gardeners, honor the tools I needed for work and then plunge my hands deep into the earth to become part of that natural alchemy that changes one form of energy into another. This honest cycle provided a comforting reassurance that nothing was really destroyed, only changed in form to nourish life elsewhere.

Little by little, I began the long, agonizing steps back towards my self—each step touching the numbness of my denial until it eventually released its grip on my soul. I began to notice my terror and as the months went by; this feeling eased into more recognizable fear, which eventually became more manageable as anxiety. As my losses continued to gain perspective, the feelings became more like concerns which were more easily understood by other members of the community. The more I shared, the more pleasantly surprised I was to find out that everybody had essentially the same story, just experienced through their own unique footprints. None of us seemed exempt from the powerful dynamics of fear, loss, rejection or abandonment and ironically, I found this comforting, even reassuring. Perhaps I wasn't quite as alone as I thought!

THE QUEST

It was another year before I felt comfortable enough to leave the safety of the community. A growing curiosity was urging me to move on and find out whom I was now and if there even was a life after survival. I applied and qualified for disability, which provided just enough resources for me to leave the community. My quest for the questions carried me through Europe, the Middle East, Australia and New Zealand until I finally arrived in India, hoping to find a direction that might guide me towards the next phase of my life. After immersing myself in the familiar rhythms of spiritual centers and ashrams, I was pleasantly surprised to discover I had already internalized a working spirituality that included some values I had chosen to keep from my parents; emerging beliefs that had been painfully birthed from disease and disability, as well as a new attitude that had shifted my external illusions of power and control towards a more internal, empowered self. Ironically, the loss of sight had provided the space for more insight, and the beginning of the end had quietly morphed into the end of my beginning. My pain had become a gift for course correction; my fear had raised the consciousness for discovering love, and disability had become my opportunity for developing new abilities. My only response to life now, was gratitude.

Fortunately, there wasn't a way back to normal behavior, once I had glimpsed what was natural. I had found reassuring hands holding mine in that space left behind after loss, while I looked for my own truth among the compost piles of Findhorn. In the spring of 1987, I returned to Tucson to begin rebuilding my life. I began with an intensive program for the blind and visually impaired so I could develop the accommodation I would need to enroll at the University of Arizona, where I received a graduate degree in Rehabilitation Counseling a few years later. At the same time, I renewed my relationship with my children, encouraging them to help me learn how to be a good father, now that I could be more present and awake.

And I heard that voice again! This time it whispered, "Say yes to this one; she is your life partner." We were driving up a long, winding hill towards Page, Arizona when I asked the thin, attractive middle-aged redhead to marry me.

She had been an incest survivor who had wrestled with her own disabilities, including attention deficit, dyslexia and hyperactivity but now I understood how disability can become our greatest gifts for transitioning fear into love, and authentic love was my final quest!

Fifteen years passed and many of the challenges remain. The cancer had resurfaced in my colon, and disquieting check-ups still confirm narrowing field vision, yet something far more sustainable had moved into that space after loss. My disabilities had revealed a new consciousness that helped me accept many of the inevitable vicissitudes of life. The gap between normal and natural had narrowed into an acceptance of all life, and earlier preoccupations with ease and comfort, had given way to simplicity and sustainability.

So, did I overcome disability or did it overcome me? The answer seems to be both! The journey has helped me realize that suffering and happiness are exercises of free will, and that all life seems to live on the doorstep of my choices. This story is my quest for truth, which I discovered among the graceful rhythms of nature while observing life of instinct and reflex. But it was the new respect I have developed for my self that has connected me to every other living thing. The only promise I can make to my readers: there is life after survival, and it rests in that space where fear and despair give way to gratitude and love.

Robert Bradford Walker is a former hospital administrator and rehabilitation counselor who is living on Whidbey Island, Washington, where he is writing his memoir, Don't Die Before You Die, *and volunteering in program development for Cancer Survivorship and Hospice Care.*

Broken Eye
Carolyn A. Dahl

Juicy yellow circles, blue zigzag lines, and hot pink triangles dance across the T-shirt my eight-year-old nephew and I just finished painting. I place another white T-shirt on the table and cover a fat, soft sponge with a layer of purple paint.

I'm about to press it to the cloth, when I feel a "ping" in my right eye, followed by a white explosion in my brain. I jump back from the table. Spider webs are crawling over the blank T-shirt, the sponge, my hand. I blink repeatedly, as if I could squeeze the strange black lines out of my eyes like dirt specks.

"Are you all right?" my nephew asks. I turn toward him. Quivering webs swirl over his cheeks, across his eyes, then race up the wall like silverfish.

"I'm not sure," is my less than comforting answer. Something is happening, but I don't know what.

"Do you see spider webs?" I ask Brett. He shakes his head. I close my right eye. Brett's face is clear, brushed with sunny morning light. Then I open that eye and close the left. His smooth skin dims, covered in a fine layer of delicate black strings. Whatever is happening to me, it's in my right eye.

I wait for pain's signal. I need pain's intensity to gauge my response. If a pain is small, I can ignore it. It may go away. A strong, persistent pain, however, means act now. This is serious. No one taught me what to do if I have an eyeful of spider webs, but absolutely no discomfort.

Without pain, my fear alarm doesn't sound. I'm just exhausted, I rationalize. Teaching art at a week-long, fast-paced conference depletes all my energy. All I need is more sleep and to relax, enjoy the vacation I'd tacked onto the end of a conference so I could visit with my sister and her family.

Besides, I'm confident my vision will clear up. I'm sure these bizarre trembling webs are nothing more than my congenital cataracts. Recently a doctor had informed me that I have had two fish-shaped cataracts in each of my eyes since birth. I'm sure it's nothing more than my fish swimming around and shaking up the vision pond. Eventually, like ripples, the congenital cataracts will settle down and the webs will disappear. I smile at Brett and tell him that we better get back to work on our T-shirts. He looks relieved. Fueled with adrenaline, we sponge, stamp, and paint three more T-shirts, then collapse on the couch for popcorn and a Disney movie.

●

Although a cool breeze from the creek blew into my bedroom all night, I know the frost on the green walls in the morning isn't really there. I close my left eye and look through my right eye, expecting to see the spider webs of yesterday crawling over the walls. I see nothing. Absolutely nothing, except a snowstorm of salt-and-pepper spots, dense as television static.

Maybe I'm still asleep, or in a dream, or a nightmare. I close one eye and see my sister's white desk and the pottery vase holding pencils like flowers. My opened, messy suitcase is in the corner. Last night's shoes lie where I kicked them off next to the door. There's the neighbor's blue house in the window with the big rock in the front yard and the fern-patterned comforter at my fingertips.

But my right eye is broken—I can't see—I can't see! I repeat the words over and over in disbelief. The fear I'd avoided yesterday gurgles inside me, then churns into a roar that could split my skin. I gasp for every breath, choke and whisper: I can't see, I can't see.

I CAN'T SEE.

I need help. I struggle to stand. I'm dizzy and unstable. Without two working eyes, I only see half of a world. I can't locate objects, or measure their shapes in one sweeping glance anymore. I can see the beginning of the door, but not the hinges on the other end, unless I turn my head. Disoriented, unsure of my sight, I rely on touch. The room moves under my fingers as if it were Braille: bumpy wall, sharp door edge, plush hall carpet, the breeze-filled stairwell.

I'm afraid I'll fall. I'm not familiar with my sister's house, nor can I remember how many steps are in a normal flight of stairs. I step down precariously; my bare feet gauge the distance between one riser to the next. I clutch the wall and follow the wallpaper pattern, which seems to shift and slide under my hands like a Ouija board.

"I need to see a doctor immediately," I say as I reach the bottom of the stairs and the kitchen where my sister Candace is sipping her morning coffee. Her eyes widen with surprise as she sees my closed eye. She rushes to the phone and dials, firing questions at me simultaneously. I turn my head to center her in my half vision and barely hear her ask, "What are your symptoms? Have you suffered a stroke? Are you blind?"

•

Balancing on the edge of the examination table, I struggle to understand the words of the Indian doctor.

"Do you have high blood pressure or diabetes? No. Were you hit in the head, or have a family history of eye problems? No. Are you very nearsighted? No. Did you see light flashes, a black curtain over part of your vision? No, no, no."

At least I don't think so. Was the white explosion I saw in my brain a light flash? Why doesn't he ask about spider webs? Am I the only one ever to see webs? Or did my artistic imagination deceive me, translating shadows and black curtains into lace?

The doctor looks deep into my eyes and increases his staccato tempo. My anxiety accelerates. "You may be having a retinal detachment," he says and suddenly rushes out the door, tossing the verdict over his shoulder like ice water. The words hit me and enter me like a newly injected drug, numbing my body. I hardly know what they mean, but the doctor's haste tells me it's the emergency I should have recognized yesterday.

Because of my ignorance, I no longer have time on my side. In the next room, the doctor speaks rapidly into the phone, while I probe my memory banks for what a retina is exactly. A sentence from an eighth-grade biology class surfaces, "Your eye is a camera and the retina is the film." But that simple analogy won't suffice. I need details, pages of medical textbook explanations to know the word's power, if it will change my life forever.

The doctor rushes back into the room, white coat flying open like low wings. "I've set up an appointment with a retinal surgeon. My nurse will give you directions to the clinic." I gulp and open my mouth to speak, but shut it when he looks into my one seeing eye and says, "You haven't time for questions. You need to hurry."

•

At the retinal clinic, the nurse calls my name. I make my sister go with me into the examination room. I can't depend on my memory for details. All day it's been thickening, growing duller and more useless as my fertile imagination feeds it images of blindness. The nurse puts dilating drops into my eye and I feel the pupil, the window to the retina, open against its will.

Quietly, the doctor, who looks like he's twenty, comes in and shakes my hand. I shoot a desperate look to my sister that says, how can I turn over my precious eye to this kid standing before me? She gives me a look of empathy and rolls her eyes.

I want to jump out of the chair, say it's all been a mistake, shake the doctor's hand, and laugh as I explain it was only my congenital cataracts playing tricks. But the doctor tilts the chair back, throws me off balance as he lowers a huge glass magnifier over the black circle of my dilated pupil. A sudden blast of bright light strikes the nerve endings deep in my eye, and I cringe as prism coronas flare inside my brain. Bending over my lowered head, his breath is warm as he presses a cold instrument above and below my eyelids, practically popping the eye out of its socket. I sniff his body like a fish I'm about to purchase, as if a particular smell could indicate if he's a conscientious surgeon.

In the dark, he moves back and forth from me to his desk to draw on round, simulated eyeball charts. With each black stroke, I know he is planning his cuts. All I can think of is the meat chart in my Betty Crocker cookbook with lines showing how to cut up beef like a puzzle or disassemble a chicken.

With the push of a button, my chair grinds slowly into an upright position. "You're in the middle of a retinal detachment all right. I see at least five rips in the retinal wall. If we had caught it earlier, we could have used a laser to reattach it. Now the eye is full of blood." His voice is soft, intimate, the way all voices are in dark doctors' offices. I don't move my body, but mentally, I grab his words out of the air, bang them on the room's walls, and hate each one for becoming mine.

"The fluid of your eye is running out as we speak, leaking into the space between the retina and its wall of nourishment." I flash back to eighth-grade biology class again. I stand with a knife poised over a cow's eye, not wanting to hurt it. The teacher grabs my hand and forces me to stab, popping the eye bag, flooding the tray with liquid.

"Your retinal wall must have had weak spots that broke open. Medically, we call the "thinning lattice degeneration" because it resembles a weaving coming apart. We'll freeze the small rips closed, then place a sponge over the biggest rip and then run a silicon band around the eye to hold everything together, like a rubber band. The silicon band and the sponge will stay in your eye forever. We'll operate tomorrow," he says.

I want to escape before he makes it permanent on a white appointment card, but my sister starts filling out the forms, while the doctor returns to his charts. I stare at him. How boyish he looks bending over the paper, like a child with a coloring book. I should ask how many of these operations he's performed, how long he's been in practice, where he went to school? No, what difference would his answers make? Do I think I can shop around while minute by minute the fluid is leaking out of my eye, collapsing my retina like a tissue?

I must find a way to surrender emotionally to his care—to trust him with my future. He does have kind denim-colored eyes. But I need a way to know him, his essence, before we meet again in the operating room.

Could I know him through his hands? Hands have habits. They become addicted to certain movements that reflect a person's character whether they're holding a spoon or a tool. I watch him closely. He positions the pencil in his fingers carefully, finds the exact spot on the paper, pauses to think, and begins to write. His body is still while the pencil moves in smooth, confident strokes from his wrist, full of an even rhythm, with no flamboyant flourishes. Every time he finishes, he returns the pencil to the desk without a sound, almost in the same location, and without the slightest roll.

Although his actions are simple, ordinary hand movements, they comfort me. I suddenly feel I can trust this young man to open up my eye. He won't hew out chunks with force like a wood worker. He will carve my eye with the skill of a Chinese paper cutter, creating cuts as delicate as the spider webs that brought me to him.

●

In my baggy blue hospital robe and paper slippers, lying on the metal-sided rolling bed, they call me Caroline, which isn't my name. But it fits; this doesn't feel at all like my life. A dark-haired anesthesiologist brings his face close to mine. At his neck a little charm on a gold chain swings like a hypnotist's tool. I ask him if it is the Chinese healing symbol, the snake. I think I remember that a snake is a powerful image in Chinese medicine, or am I confusing it with the coiled snakes on the caduceus, the insignia symbolizing a physician in Western culture? It doesn't matter. All I want is a final vision of beauty, a protective talisman to take into the darkness in which he's about to plunge me.

"We'll take care of you," he smiles and releases the juice of sleep into my veins. I start to drop down the black hole as he laughs to my doctor, "I just put her out, you have time for a scotch." Panic arches and pushes my consciousness up through the descending fog long enough to see the gold snake change into a simple S-clasp of a necklace before the hospital lights go out.

My drugged mind swims, twists, and rolls in voices I can't answer. Although I am technically unconscious and subdued by waves of chemical sleep, my body's visceral intelligence remains alert. Above my limp body, my doctor inserts the local anesthesia needle into my head and eye. My facial muscles numb and my eye stops moving.

With another set of chemicals, they return me to consciousness. I am on the operating table. As the glare of the hospital lights blasts my face, I wonder if my decision to be awake during the surgery was wise. Why did I think I wanted to see the sterile white room, the masked figures in ghostly gowns circling me, or feel the clamp lock my head in place, or the pain of the IV pulling at my tiny veins?

A large piece of equipment lowers into position above me and a rush of claustrophobia threatens to take my breath. Then in the background, I hear classical music. A nice, andante movement begins to sand away the edges of my panic. My heartbeat slows. The room fills with music, and my own heart joins in, beeping from the monitor like a tiny piccolo of life.

With my unbroken eye covered with a towel and the IV dripping happy juice, I am awake and strangely calm. The doctor is behind my head. I imagine my eye sitting on a platter as he works, like St. Lucia holding eyeballs in her hand on a Catholic prayer card I once saw as a child. The shape of a knife crosses my vision and I realize that I am witnessing my own surgery. The room resonates with murmuring conversation, the swelling music, and instruments ringing in the metal trays. With minimal commands, the doctor orchestrates the operation. I feel his skill and concentration transform into a state of flow, which I recognize as the same that I enter when I work in my art studio.

While he works on my tiny eye, I swing through levels of consciousness. I come to the surface to answer, "Yes, I'm fine," and then drop away on violin strings for another half hour to remember the red tulips in last year's garden. Somewhere between revising a poem I'd started, and thinking about the drawings in my studio, he says, "This will hurt." It does. Why, I wonder? Did he pop my eye back into the socket, or pull the stitches extra tight?

Full of the energy that comes when something dreaded is over, I am talkative and ask to see the sponge that saved my sight. I need to touch the foreign object that is now inside of me, need to know if it is colored, or full of holes like my printing sponges. He dangles a white, snakelike tube before my good eye. I didn't expect it to look scratchy like pipe insulation. My mind rejects it as uncomfortable, then reels the thought back in for fear my body won't accept it.

"May I have a piece of it as a souvenir?" I ask. My doctor smiles and cuts off a section and slips it into my hand. I hold it tightly. "Thank you doctor...for everything....for my sight."

They roll me into recovery. The anesthesia is disappearing and my apple juice tastes tart and harsh on my tongue. Under the white bandage covered with a hard plastic guard plate, my broken eye sees nothing but brilliant bursts of purple color. I have no idea yet how much vision I have lost, or what being "nearly unsighted" in one eye might mean to my life as an artist. I think of my studio. Will I be able to finish the detailed drawings pinned to the back wall if I can't connect lines? The doctor said I may have scarring, puckers in my retina from the holes, or large blind spots.

"Perhaps," he said, "You will never see a perfectly straight vertical line again."

●

In two days, I learned the doctor was right; my vertical lines would never be straight again. But I could see. I finished my drawings and resumed most of my former activities. Instead of being devastated by the loss, I've become fascinated with the strange visual world my damaged sight adds to my creative life. But sometimes, the hump of the sponge stitched into my eye bumps my eyelid, or I feel the rubber band stretch as my eye turns in the socket, and I remember the day I lost my perfect sight.

Carolyn A. Dahl is the author of Natural Impressions *(Watson-Guptill) and* Transforming Fabric *(Krause Publications). She was an award winner in the PEN Texas nonfiction competition. She frequently appears on Home and Garden Television and PBS programs. www.carolyndahlstudio.com*

Portal
Michael Constantine McConnell

"Stay very still," the doctor said. "If you move while I'm doing this, if you so much as flinch or cough, you may never walk again." I held my breath. I could hear the pressure of the moment chime through my bones when the needle scraped my spine. I still flinch at the shrill whine of fork into plate or a sheet of aluminum foil being slowly torn in half.

I'd been watching cartoons on the television nested in one of the ceiling-corners of my room in Detroit Children's Hospital. I was about a week into the diagnostic phase of my extended visit. There'd been process and schedule involved in the other tests—at least I knew that once the tests begun in the morning, another would follow and so on until the doctors were done with me for the afternoon. I remember the test where my torso and head lay inside of a tube that made loud noises, and the test where wires taped to my arms sent lightning into my shoulders. But the spinal tap was a different story. The doctor snuck in like a gypsy and thieved fluid from the spire that holds my body together.

I exhaled and snapped out of my daydream and a past I hadn't thought about in fifteen years. I stood in a hospital room in the Shriners Burn Center in Shreveport, Louisiana. We'd made the trip out from Tyler, Texas, a few hours away. When I say "we," I mean other players from my football team and a few of our cheerleaders and members of the drill squad, as well as our counterparts from the Mississippi team, Hinds Junior College, whom the Tyler Apaches would battle the following day in the Shrine Bowl. Shriners led us from ward to ward, room to room, child to child, to offer hope and encouragement to severely burned and crippled children; most of their smiles seemed oblivious to the burden of their damaged bodies.

But a child named Christopher didn't smile. He didn't have lips or what most would recognize as a mouth. Until a Shriner wandered into his room and told me the patient's name, I didn't even know if the little human in the bed before me was a boy or a girl; most of the skin on his body—all but the forearm and hand on his left side—had melted then hardened into a shell of scar tissue. His eyes, however, remained intact, brilliant, and steady as stone pillars. The other football players signed little rubber footballs and set them in his lap before moving on to the next room, but I couldn't take my eyes off of Christopher's strong eyes. They invited me to remember where I came from.

Guillam-Barre Syndrome is a difficult vocabulary word for a five year old. A virus that attacks the central nervous system, Guillam-Barre claimed me as one of its rare victims—about one in every one-hundred-thousand people. I'd woken up one morning, and keeping my balance was too physically demanding. I felt as if I were stumbling through a funhouse with moving floors. By the end of the night, I couldn't support my own weight, and my mother rushed me to the hospital. Two days later, I couldn't feed myself, and my feet and legs felt like they'd been twisted into a thin, long single spiral.

I had to adjust to the discomfort and absence of motor skills and coordination. I had to get used to my weak legs that hung limp off of a wheelchair. I had to get used to seeing my mother weep when she could no longer hold courage in her smile. She didn't have a husband, only me—her only son—and a job waitressing at the "Coney Island" restaurant in the mall on the east side of Detroit. She would come to the hospital reeking of chili and hot dogs and mustard; then her second shift began. She'd wheel me up and down the halls, accelerating on my demand.

"Mommy, do it again," I'd say, again and again. "Faster." When she'd become completely exhausted by the end of the evening, she'd put me to bed and sit for hours in the room with me. I couldn't sleep very well in the hospital, but I'd lay still in bed, pretending to sleep while she sobbed herself asleep. I couldn't rest until she rested, until she slept in her chair and a nurse covered her with a blanket.

"Does he have family nearby?" I quietly asked a Shriner, who motioned me outside of Christopher's room.

"His grandmother comes to see him about once a week," said the Shriner, shaking his head. "But she's very old, and the trip up here from Baton Rouge is hard on her. Christopher's parents died in the fire."

I walked back into his room. By this time, all of the other football players and cheerleaders and drill squad members had made their full rounds and were congregated in the hospital's front lobby. Christopher sat where I'd left him, and his eyes picked me up where they'd left me. Those eyes and his left arm were the only things that the fire hadn't hurt—but I could tell that something undamaged thrived inside of him. I couldn't speak, not even to say "hello." I wanted to tell him that everything would be alright; I wanted to tell him that he'd grow up to be healthy and normal, and he could play football like me, but what could I say that one of the others hadn't said? I used to be like you? But I made it through this, so can you? I think that I realized for the first time in my life the inadequacy of words, and even now, I look back and question my silence. Sometimes, when someone is in a really bad state, you never know what effect words will have. You never know whether a freshly handicapped child will receive encouragement with hope or resignation. His young reality hinged at the apex of a balance few people can understand. Even the doctors were unsure of Christopher's recovery.

My recovery came quicker than the doctors had expected. I remember revolting against the wheelchair. I remember my moment of choice, my moment of resolve. I remember sneaking off alone to an empty visiting room, where I'd perform small exercises. I'd push myself up out of the wheelchair a few inches and let some of the weight fall on my weak legs, which would immediately buckle. Days and days of this activity proved effective. After about a week, I could stand up and let go of my wheelchair for a second or two. A few days after that, I could stand and take a step forward before falling back into my wheelchair. A few days after that, I could take two steps.

On Valentines Day, 1979, after being confined to a wheelchair for over a month, I took my first steps for the second time in my life. The nurses threw a party for the children and parents. My mother arrived late at the hospital after working a double shift that day. All day, I had waited patiently, nurturing a secret that belonged to me and nobody else. When she walked into the ward lobby and the party, I couldn't wait anymore; I pushed myself up with my arms and stood shakily in front of the wheelchair that had substituted as my legs for over a month. A hush fell over the floor and drop-jawed nurses stepped out of the path between my mother, who had dropped a bouquet of flowers and a box of chocolate on the floor at her feet, and me. I swung my body and lifted one of my legs, catching my weight and balance when my foot retouched the ground. I took another step. I wasn't holding on to the wheelchair anymore, and the world advanced in slow-motion frames. I took another step. I looked up. My mother held her hands out to me, motioning for me to walk the rest of the way, assuring me that everything was going to be alright. Tears poured in steady streams out of her eyes. I lunged out a few more jerky steps and collapsed into her arms.

"Happy Valentines Day, Mommy."

The memories hit me all at once, and a tear fell out of my eye. It wasn't a tear of pity, and Christopher knew that—I just know that he knew. It wasn't for him, and it wasn't for me; it was ours; it was something we shared. A Shriner walked into the room to tell me that it was time to get back on the bus, that visiting hours were over. In a gesture of parting, I spread my hand over Christopher's good hand—the unburned one on the left side of his body, and five perfect little fingers grabbed one of mine and squeezed tightly.

Michael Constantine McConnell's most recent poems, palindromes, and short stories have appeared or are forthcoming in the Backwards City Review, Jabberwock Review, The Bitter Oleander, Style, *and* 32 Poems. *Michael teaches writing and devoutly studies the 20-button Anglo concertina.*

PART THREE

Fresh Tracks

Another's Disability

Fresh Tracks
Samantha Ducloux Waltz

"Mom, Mt. Hood got new snow last night. I just heard it on the radio. Want to go to Meadows and make fresh tracks?"

I turned from the stove where I was cooking breakfast, a Saturday ritual to appease my single working mom guilt. Here was an opportunity to spend quality time with my seventeen-year-old son Ben and ski powder in mid-April. But I had a mile-high stack of compositions to read for the high-school English classes I taught, a refrigerator growing green stuff on myriad leftovers, a pile of bills that had to be paid before looming due dates.

"It's Saturday. We still have tomorrow to catch up on stuff. You need this," Ben argued, grabbing a piece of bacon.

I did need this. My body was so tense I could pull a muscle just by cocking my head. I should have known my sensitive son could see it. When stress sometimes overwhelmed me he would intuit my despair and grab me in a bear hug. If I dressed to the nines for an important date with my boyfriend Rick, he'd give me a wolf whistle. He was a counselor as much as I in our occasional late-night conversations over hot chocolate. "You load your snowboard and my skis," I said. "I'll pack a lunch."

Within minutes we were off to Mt. Hood Meadows Ski Resort two hours away. Ben punched on the car radio and I hummed to the rhythm of a rock band as we headed out. The first hour we filled with conversation about school projects, his friends, ideas for summer vacation. I began to relax.

Then, out of nowhere, a police car turned its siren on behind me. Hadn't I seen the speed limit sign, she asked when she pulled me over. Her eyes were merciless as she handed me a ticket for a staggering amount.

No, I hadn't seen the sign. When did they sneak a 40 MPH zone in the middle of the 55 MPH stretch of highway 26? As if my mood had not been adequately squelched, a damp veil of fog settled over the highway, and more snow, not predicted, began to fall as we wound up the mountain. The road grew slick. Cars and SUVs, their snow tires removed since the season was all but over, slid precariously. I hunched over the steering wheel, pushing away a mental image of our Corolla upside down in a ditch.

"Don't worry, Mom," Ben said. "I can put on the chains."

I cautiously turned the wheel to the right to join the vehicles chaining up along the shoulder. The car slid left across the road, nosed into a snow bank, miraculously without hitting other vehicles, and dropped its wheels into a shallow ditch. Ben climbed out to survey our predicament; I followed to give what assistance I could.

"I'll try to get on the chains so we can back out," Ben said hopefully.

My son, the optimist. I bit my lip in frustration. We'd need a tow truck.

A woman approached and offered to pay Ben if he would chain up her car stalled out on a slight incline nearby. He said he'd help her for free and headed toward her Buick twenty feet away. As I opened my own trunk for chains something slammed me from behind, doubling me over the Corolla's trunk.

Before I could call out for Ben, a scream split the air. I turned and saw my son lying on a snow-covered rise. I struggled to him, the sharp pain in my back keeping me in a half-crouch. Both his legs jutted at odd angles from his knees and a pool of blood stained the snow scarlet where he lay. My own injury forgotten in a stab of fear for my son, I took his hands. We held each other with our eyes for ten long minutes, both of us shivering from the damp, icy air, and from shock. In sobbing gasps, Ben said over and over, "My legs, my legs—I can't believe this happened." And, "Let this be a dream, just a dream." Sometimes he said, only, "Mom?"

And I said, "I'm here. Hang on. Help is coming."

People brought blankets, called for an ambulance, murmured to each other, their conversation a muted buzz around me. A police car arrived, ironically the policewoman who had issued my ticket. A man approached, the driver of the car that had struck me a glancing blow, then hit another car, crushing Ben's legs between the vehicles. He nervously assured me of adequate insurance. Insurance? I just wanted my son to live.

A young man carrying a medical bag came up to us. "I'm an emergency tech," he said. "Officially off work, but I have my bag."

I sobbed with relief as at last I released Ben's hands. Someone offered me a lap robe and I wrapped myself in its fleecy warmth, praying frantically while the ET cut away clothing and applied tourniquets. An ambulance arrived, then another. Paramedics worked many more long minutes stabilizing Ben, preparing him for a cautious drive to ZigZag, the first town off the mountain. A Life Flight helicopter would be waiting there. As the medics loaded him he raised his head from the gurney just enough to look around at his attendants. "Thank you, everyone, for helping me so much," he said.

Perhaps I'd been moaning aloud, though I was still oblivious to my own misery. Medics from a second ambulance strapped me to a gurney and loaded me into their ambulance. "You're doing fine," one said as we drove cautiously down the mountain.

"No I'm not," I replied, gritting my teeth against screams of pain and terror. Then I thought of Ben's silent struggle back there on the mountain. His struggle to not only remain conscious, but to thank those who helped him. I gathered my own courage. At the hospital a nurse wheeled Ben to me on his way into surgery. "Hi, Mom," he said hoarsely and I cried with relief to see him alive.

I was x-rayed, diagnosed with a fractured sacrum, and given pain medication. I'd used Rick's number as my emergency contact when I was admitted, and when he arrived I clung to him, sobbing. Ben would be in surgery for hours more and I wanted to see my other children. To hug them fiercely. Thank God they had chosen not to go skiing with us. How much I might have lost.

Rick took me home to my daughter and younger son who were as pale and tearful as me, and we returned to the hospital together. Late in the evening the surgeon showed us Ben's x-rays. His clavicle, broken in the fall, would heal without treatment. But stark black and white photographs of his legs revealed completely shattered tibia and fibula, the bone fragments large, irregular chunks, like white bark dust except for a few long shards of splintered bone. Nerves had been destroyed, muscle and connective tissue damaged beyond the possibility of complete healing, circulation so impaired that a serious infection could easily develop. Metal rods now ran from knee to foot. The surgeon thought he could save the right leg. He felt less confident about the left.

My knees buckled and my breath caught in my throat. My son. My wonderful, beautiful son.

I knew how much my back hurt. I couldn't imagine what Ben was enduring. Day after day he lay in the hospital, oozing fluids soaking the bandages on both his legs within an hour of application. I would hold his hand as he lay awake, his legs cramping so badly he wanted to scream, unable to have any more medication. Sometimes I read to him, sometimes we talked of the accident, angry at Ben's fate and fearing for his future, sometimes we cried together. Mental images of Ben with one trouser leg pinned at the thigh or a stiff prosthetic swinging wide as he walked haunted me. For days I wandered through the house, picking up a stray sock here, a snowboarding magazine there. "He's alive," I would say aloud, pressing the item to my chest.

If only my pain medication would deaden my anguished mind along with the severe ache in my back. I journaled obsessively about my concerns for Ben, and leaned on the support of my other children, friends, and especially Rick. The fourth day when I entered Ben's hospital room, he comforted me with, "Hi, Mom, thanks for getting me those good snowboarding boots with thick soles. The car hit right between my knees and ankles. If the boots hadn't made me taller my knees would have been smashed too."

When Ben was released from the hospital after ten days, he went to the home of his father and stepmother. He required the care of two adults to turn him and I, a single mom with a broken back, had to admit that I could not care adequately for my suffering child. His father's oblique comments suggesting in some way I was partly responsible for the accident heightened my anguish.

After three more weeks of healing, Ben wanted to come home. A cousin flew out from Ohio to assist with his care. I returned to work part time to keep a paycheck coming. Ben weaned himself from the pain medications because he couldn't stand the feeling of being "half there." We watched his legs slowly heal, marveling at his good disposition through so much suffering. Bits of muscle turned dark and blue, resembling pieces of plum. On visits to the orthopedic clinic, the doctor snipped off the dead tissue and discarded it in a plastic receptacle. The swelling in Ben's legs receded, revealing a bone fragment protruding from one leg. The doctor took a tool that looked like cutters to trim the hoof of a horse and snipped off the bone fragment. Each time I wanted to cry out, to vomit, to do something, anything, to take these horrors away from my son. Sometimes he pressed his lips in grim silence. Sometimes he reached for my hand and comforted me.

Ben spent hours in a wheelchair now. Rick replaced the three steps from our kitchen to our garage with a sturdy wheelchair ramp and Ben ventured out for car rides. He returned to school for a day. His left leg was healing without complications and we rejoiced. Then the shin of his right leg began to sag, sucked air when he lifted it, gurgled when he set it down. The terror-breeding specter of amputation roamed our house. When I thought life could not get more difficult, I learned that Rick was seeing another woman. He left our lives forever. How would I survive the nightmare that had begun that day on the mountain and now included a broken heart? And yet, if Ben could go on, minute by minute, hour by hour, how could I not?

Ben's doctor referred us to a surgeon who specialized in "saving limbs." The surgeon took an abdominal muscle that stretched from Ben's pubic bone to his rib cage, reshaped it to resemble a kidney bean, and attached it to the veins and arteries above what was left of Ben's calf muscle. He added antibiotic beads to a remaining gap, a skin graft from Ben's thigh over the new calf muscle, and a shunt to a vein near Ben's heart for injection of massive doses of antibiotics. We wouldn't know for two weeks if the graft had taken so that Ben would have a chance to keep his leg. He explained to his visiting rugby team that under the bandages his leg looked like the doctor had sewn a big, pink pork chop onto it and then stapled cheesecloth over it. His humor got us through another day.

The muscle graft took, the antibiotics worked. A bone graft with bone marrow from Ben's pelvis finished the job. I knew of the excruciating pain in his pelvis only from the beads of sweat on his forehead and his deathly pallor when he had to move from wheelchair to bed. This son had been the most athletic of my children. Now he astonished me with the life he created for himself. We lived on a hill that he had climbed a hundred times, carrying his skateboard up and then streaking down, a flash of boy and color. Now he wheeled down the ramp and outside to challenge that hill. Day after day for a month he struggled up it until he could wheel himself around the block, a slow-motion film clip of man and sweat. Then he would put a VW repair manual in his lap, wheel himself down the ramp to the garage, put the repair manual on the ground under the rear bumper of ancient VW Beetle, slide onto the concrete alongside it, and work on "Floyd."

Eventually Ben traded his wheelchair for crutches, an agonizing proposition. With me there to help if needed, he put weight on his legs for the first time in five months. After several more months he was able to walk again without crutches, albeit with a slight shuffle.

Every day he lived his self-proclaimed credo, "Learn to accept who you are, what limitations you have in the life that fate has dealt you, and go for whatever you want." Not that it was easy. He told me during one of our late night refrigerator raids how separate and alone and discouraged he often felt. He graduated high school, but his senior year seemed long and lonely. He'd missed a year and many of his friends had gone on to college. Pep rallies and homecoming courts seemed unbearably trivial. He skated and snowboarded again, but found that even short intervals proved painful and nerve damage had robbed him of his flexibility. When he dated he felt self-conscious about his scarring.

Still he faced steadily forward. One summer he was a volunteer counselor at a youth camp and somehow completed a mile run. Afterward, those who watched cried along with him at his victory. He studied Autocad at the community college and worked part time using it, he restored Volkswagens, he completed a college program in furniture making and designed and built fine furniture.

Best of all, one New Year's Eve he met a girl who had a spark he hadn't seen in anyone else. Nearly three years later they exchanged vows. Alicia looked into his eyes and said beautiful, tender things to this man who would be her husband. One line in particular etched itself into my heart. "I love your legs and the things that they have endured in order to bring you here to stand in front of me today." At that moment, as I took the hand of my own new husband, I relinquished my son to this wonderful young woman, having learned from him how to more fully live. It had been ten years since he left his blood on the snow of Mt. Hood. We were all setting off to make fresh tracks.

Samantha Ducloux Waltz is a freelance writer in Portland, Oregon. Her personal essays have appeared in four volumes of the Cup of Comfort *series,* Midlife Clarity, Horse Crazy, The Healing Touch of Horses, *and* The Christian Science Monitor. *She has also published adult nonfiction and juvenile fiction under the names Samantha Ducloux and Samellyn Wood. Her hero is her son, Benjamin Wood.*

Joshua's Rainbows
Lisa Mae Menold-Hochstetler

On December 2, 1997, I gave birth to twins—a beautiful, delicate little girl with blue eyes and dark brown hair we named Joy, and her tiny brother, topped with copper penny red hair, Joshua. I hardly got to spend our early days together, sick with phlebitis in my uterus and then a staph infection that kept us apart. When we were finally released from the hospital to go home with Daddy and eleven-month-old Matthew, I had an I.V. in my arm and my healthy babies.

1998 was not an easy year for us. I had three babies in 1997, Matthew in January, the twins in December, and became a full-time stay-at-home Mom, while Marcus worked full-time in a law firm library and went to graduate school full-time for his Masters in Library Sciences. In fact, I do not remember much of 1998; bottles and diapers seemed to consume much of my memory of that time. I remember when they were sick, when they did their firsts, but that was it.

Joshua was always different from the rest. He liked to be held and cuddled, just like the other two, but he was more laid back, more easy going than his demanding princess twin Joy or playful Matthew. I always called him my status-quo baby. The one baby who went with the flow, Joshua was good-natured about most everything. The one thing Josh really liked was his routine, especially at night when I would read and later sing to the four of them. His favorite lullaby was "For Baby," a beautiful song by John Denver. At night, I would sit in the Amish hickory rocker, hold him, and sing, "I'll walk in the rain by your side, I'll cling to the warmth your tiny hand, I'll do anything to help you understand, I love you more than anybody can."

Even then, I doubt if Joshua or I understood how that last line would ring true, that I'll love you more than anybody can. Joshua amazed me in so many ways. He was brilliant, adorable, and like a typical redhead, he had a temper. There were days when I felt totally overwhelmed, when I just had to take a timeout and cry for myself. When the twins were teething eyeteeth at nine months, I had each of them in snugglies on my hips. I bounced them for eight hours, just waiting for their father to walk through the door so I could run out and just leave the noise for a little while. I'll never forget when all three had the stomach flu and were projectile vomiting in three different directions. Those were trying times. When I've gone through the difficult situations, I think back to that time and remind myself that I will get over whatever small hurdles stand in my way.

When Baby Hope was born, Joshua had just turned two and wanted nothing to do with her. A month before, right before his birthday, he received vaccinations and had one more than his twin for some reason we never could understand. I was used to the typical fever and fussiness of vaccinations, but not thirty-six hours of a little boy screaming, feverish and totally inconsolable. After that, we began to see his behavior go downhill. Josh was no longer the happy, cheerful baby who was so easygoing.

If a sibling interrupted his favorite television shows, he'd throw a temper tantrum that was beyond anything we had ever experienced. He had obsessions, certain toys that he carried with him always. He became obstinate, and what's more, he quit communicating with us as he had. No longer speaking in full sentences, I was lucky to get him to utter two to three word phrases, and before Hope was one, he was parroting everything I asked back to me. I'd ask the pediatricians, and they said it was nothing. Each said that he was just upset because his younger sister was getting his attention, and they based all of his behavioral issues on being a redhead in the throws of the terrible twos who needed preschool and socialization.

The little boy I sung to at night, screamed if I sung now, "And the wind will whisper your name to me, little birds will sing along in time, leaves will bow down when you walk by, and morning bells will chime." I remember crying as I held him one night, trying so desperately to console him as I always had, and wishing for the baby that I held months ago, the baby that cooed when I sang, whose eyes always met mine as I did, now rarely looked up at me unless he was screaming. No little birds would sing for him, no rainbows could be seen in the dark gloomy skies, something was wrong, but I didn't know what.

When he turned three, we started him in pre-school, and even then, nothing changed in Joshua's behavior. In some ways, he was worse. I wouldn't find out until a year later that the director of the preschool and a speech therapist knew all along what was wrong with my little boy, but didn't bother to tell me.

That fall, after a very trying summer when I only got a few hours of sleep a night with Joshua, he started preschool at another location, and the teacher said to me within the first week, "Something is wrong with him, you need to have him tested." I argued with her, telling her she didn't know what she was talking about, and that she didn't know how to deal with him.

She listed her credentials, then said she was doing me a favor by telling me and walked away, obviously refusing to deal with a mother in denial. I called my pediatrician, who saw us that day and then referred us to a psychologist he knew. When she saw Joshua, she took him to another room for an hour and tested him, then brought him back to us.

"Joshua has Asperger's Syndrome, which is a mild form of autism," she said.

"What syndrome and mild form of what?" asked my husband. We sat there in shock.

For the next week, I would cry alone at night, privately grieving, feeling as if my boy would never be the same as he once was to me. He was no longer perfect and brilliant—he was autistic. This couldn't be. This was the baby who knew his alphabet-both upper and lowercases-by eighteen months. This child read three letter words and could memorize lines from shows and programs. This couldn't be my son they were talking about, or could it?

I began to take him to see doctors. One after the other told me the same thing, suggested other methods of treatment. I scoped out schools and sobbed at the lower functioning children they meant to put him with instead of his siblings who were his peer group. Finally, someone told me about the Autism Support Preschool through Youngstown City Schools. I called and discovered that classroom was in the elementary school only a mile from us. When I visited the classroom, I had a hard time keeping it together. The teacher and the aides could see how visibly shaken I was, how I needed some support and help for Joshua. What's more, I needed to be told that he was going to be all right, that he was going to make it as long as I didn't give up.

At one point, I thought I might. Our insurance company dropped everything for Joshua. They refused to pay for the neurologist, the medication, the psychologist, and would not cover speech or occupational therapy. I was angry. Because of our income, we didn't qualify for Medicaid, we had to go through Social Security and they had refused us twice already. Another mom of an autistic boy from the same classroom took me to the Social Security office and told them I needed help. She helped me fill out the forms, told me it had to be done, and finally, on the third try, we were given a meager cash benefit, but no medical assistance, which meant no external therapies other than the fifteen minutes once a month that he got at school.

Frustrated, I went to the school and sought out the Occupational Therapist and the Speech Therapist. I looked at them across the table where they were eating lunch and said to them, "Teach me to do what you do."

"What?" asked Jan, the Occupational Therapist, certain that she didn't hear me right.

"I want you to teach me to do what you do. The insurance won't pay for his therapy. You guys are spread too thin to give him all the time he needs. I want you to teach me to do what you do and send homework home every week so we can work on it daily."

The two sat there in shock, the bites of food in their mouths half-chewed. They had never had a parent come in with a request such as that. As they swallowed, they realized I was more serious about this than anything else in the world. Nothing else mattered to me. I had to get Josh help, and if the outside world wouldn't do it, then I would. And I did. If he failed, it wouldn't be for my lack of trying. All I wanted was for him to succeed, to show the rest of them what I already knew—Joshua was brilliant.

Josh would go to preschool for six hours a day four days a week and I would spend an hour a night at the dining room table with him doing the "homework" the Occupational Therapist and Speech Therapist had sent home with him. I taught him to keyboard since his handwriting was a deficit for him, and Joshua flourished with the computer. He could do anything on the computer, and at one point, installed a printer that neither of his parents could install successfully. I spent hours reading with Joshua, determined that the same language barrier that plagued these children, wouldn't do likewise to my son, so we read together for an hour a night before bed.

Juggling Joshua and his three other siblings has always been difficult for me. I could not work outside of the home and manage a family as well, so I opted to give up my hopes of returning to work as a human resources headhunter, and be the stay-at-home mom I was supposed to be. While the other children made leaps and bounds with their development, I watched closely for every ounce of progress on Joshua's part. Parents of autistic children, regardless of where they land on the spectrum, note accomplishments that other parents of regular education children would take for granted.

For instance, I remember the first sentence Joshua ever spoke after his diagnosis: "Mom, I can't find my Barney pillow." I remember his first word, it was Mama, but his first sentence, that memory I hold much dearer, as it took over a year to get him to say it.

Joshua was making leaps and bounds in his progress and by the time his twin was ready to go to kindergarten, his preschool teacher and other supervisors in the program decided Joshua was not ready. But that didn't stop his twin, his champion, from her adamant disagreement that Joshua couldn't make it in kindergarten. No, Joy was determined that he was going WITH her to kindergarten, and wouldn't let up. Every day she asked, "Mommy, is Joshy going with me to Kindergarten? I want Joshy to go with me to Kindergarten. He can read better than anyone in preschool, he's smart, he can do it."

Finally, I told the teacher I wanted Josh mainstreamed into kindergarten the following year, and she balked at my request. I said, test him. They did, and still said no. The school being in fiscal emergency wouldn't pay an aide to accompany him to class, and we knew he couldn't do it well enough on his own.

That week, the board of education had a seminar on Dr. Spencer Johnson's book *Who Moved My Cheese?* and gave each parent a copy of the book. I went home and read the metaphor of the maze and the little mice and boys that ran through it and thought, maybe it's time to move where the cheese is. So, I began to investigate and found out that if we moved a half-hour away, across the border into Pennsylvania, that Joshua could have medical assistance, Social Security, and a wrap-around agency would provide his classroom aide and his behavioral specialist.

Our family wasn't pleased with the move, but their approval didn't matter. All that mattered was Joshua's success. The other three children would make it, regardless of where they were, all of them read two grade levels above their peers and were academically superior in their classroom environments. Dealing with the school district in Sharon, Pennsylvania was like night and day to that of Youngstown, Ohio. Finally, I had help, medical assistance and a child on medication. At most, prior to the move, I was getting two and a half hours of sleep per night, keeping Joshua from destroying the house when he'd get up in the middle of the night. When his doctor put him on medication, I began to sleep as Joshua did. Everything seemed a little brighter and a little more hopeful than it had in recent months.

A few months after the move, we were in a new home, and while I was upstairs helping to put children to bed, Josh wanted to sit on my lap again in the rocker. I cuddled him as I had and he looked up into my eyes and in his sweet voice he sang, "And I'll sing you the songs of the rainbow," reminding me of the beautiful lullaby I used to sing him. Happily, I obliged him and sang with him, "The whisper of the joy that is mine, leaves will bow down when you by, and morning bells will chime." I sang that song through twice that night as tears fell down my face, my eyes failing to hold them back. I didn't want to put Joshua into his bed that night, I just wanted to hold him, my baby, who gave me more hope in those few minutes, than anyone had in the last two years.

That year, Joshua spent the first half of his day in an Autism Support classroom that fine-tuned his classroom behavioral issues, that augmented his speech therapy to daily speech therapy, and in the afternoon, he went to Kindergarten with his twin, Joy, thrilling her. Every day we would see improvements in Joshua and we really believed he would make it. In the first grade, Joshua joined his twin Joy in the class and is fully mainstreamed today. We still have our behavioral hurdles, we still have toileting issues and destruction problems but we know that he's going to make it. After all, how many first graders leave the classroom once a day just for third grade reading?

Does this mean my work is done? By far, it's not. We have a long way to go, but we'll make it. When the children were little, I made a rule that "Can't" was a bad word and not to be uttered in the house. When I hear it spoken, all I have to do is shoot a look at the offending child for him to recite as they were taught as toddlers, "I can do anything I want to do, if I work hard, believe in myself and never give up."

Every week as a room mother, I'm in the classroom with one of my children. It amazes me when I peek into Joshua and Joy's classroom door's window and see Joshua interacting and doing his work just like any other child in the room. Joy keeps an eye on him and acts as a social buffer for Joshua, and she is so happy that he's there with her, but we know that there are times when it's hard for her to have her brother in her classroom. When I think of the twins, I remember the champion who wouldn't relent and the little boy who tried his best to be like everyone else.

Mainstream education isn't without its own set of complications and issues, of fears and triumphs, so I do my best to be there for all four of the children. Reminding myself of the promise I made them when I sang to them in my arms, "I'll be there when you're feeling down, to kiss away the tears if you cry, I'll share with you all the happiness I've found, a reflection of the love in your eyes." John Denver's "For Baby" may have been meant for his own baby, but it truly was for all of mine, especially Joshua. Some people find strength and inspiration from books, the Bible, or church. What builds me up on our worst days is the memory of a simple song and the look in a little boy's eyes that wanted me to sing to him again, knowing that just like then, we'd overcome whatever hurdles stood in our way, and the resolution would be just as rewarding if not more as that moment.

Lisa Mae Menold-Hochstetler, graduate of Ashland University, lives in Seattle, Washington, with her husband Marcus and four children. She has been published in 911: The Day America Cried, A Gathered Stillness: Devotional Thoughts from the Malone College Family; *and* True Romance Magazine. *She was a winner of the 2005 Northwest Playwrights Competition.*

Mario Pieroni: A Blind Man's Journey
Susan Schenck Stall

People have told me that I am an extraordinary person. They have said they cannot imagine how I achieved all I did. I don't feel so special. In fact, talk like that makes me uncomfortable. I have read about many people who did accomplish amazing things in their lives. But, I don't believe I have ever done anything that was truly extraordinary. I may have done some daring things in my younger days. Like the time my brother and I climbed to the top of the YWCA building that was under construction near our house in Muncie, Indiana.

It was during the summer and I was home from school in Indianapolis. The neighborhood kids were all talking about the skyscraper being built not far from our house. The new Y building was going to be four stories high, a real skyscraper by Muncie standards. By the time I got home from school, the steel girders that made up the framework of the building were in place. To us kids, it looked like a giant jungle gym had been erected for us to climb. One warm Saturday afternoon we decided to scale the structure. As we walked to the deserted construction site, I kept the fingers of my right hand lightly touching Charlie's left elbow. We were so used to walking like this that neither of us realized we were touching. When we arrived at the edge of the construction site, we all stopped. I felt Charlie's whole body bend backwards as he looked to the top of the steel frame that would soon become the new Y.

"How does it look, Charlie?"

"Mario, it looks like it's just begging us to climb it. You ready?"

"If you can do it, Charlie, so can I. Let's go!"

We climbed a tall ladder to reach the first level of horizontal beams. I climbed just behind Charlie. The ladder sagged slightly beneath us with each step we took. One of our friends climbed behind me and the ladder dipped even more. We were all quiet as we climbed. Sweat trickled down the center of my back. I concentrated on matching Charlie's progress rung for rung. We stepped off the ladder onto wooden planks that created a crude walkway. I kept my hand on Charlie's shoulder. Each board bent under our weight as though we were crossing a sort of suspended bridge.

When we came to the first steel girder, Charlie said, "Okay Mario, it's time to get down on all fours for this part. Keep one hand on my hip, so you'll stay on the beam."

I carefully lowered myself until my knees were side by side on the twelve-inch wide beam. The metal felt warm to my touch, as the summer sun beat down on us I placed my left hand on Charlie's hip and crawled behind him like a three-legged dog. Eventually, we reached the top of the building. I don't know how we did it, but we did. I wasn't frightened at all back then. Now just the thought of our adventure scares me.

When we reached the top, all of us boys sat down on the girder side by side. We laughed as we let our legs dangle in the open air. We turned our faces to the sun, basking in the glory of our accomplishment. One of the boys called out, "Look Charlie, you can see your house over there." Another friend said, "Yeah, and over that way you can see the steeple of the big Presbyterian church downtown."

"Hey, Mario. Listen, I'm going to spit," my brother said. There was a long moment of silence before I heard his spit ping off a piece of sheet metal on the ground below us. I could not stop the shiver of excitement that coursed through my body. My fingers and toes tingled as though I'd had a near miss. When Charlie saw me shiver, he placed his hand on my arm to steady me. We all cheered and began to spit from our lofty perches.

One of the neighbors saw us climb that skyscraper. He went to see my Dad. "Tony, you are a darned fool to let that boy of yours run all over the neighborhood. I can't believe you let him climb that new YWCA building."

"I appreciate your concern, I really do. I have told Charles to be careful."

"I am not talking about Charlie, for God's sake. I am talking about Mario. What if he had fallen off that building?"

"You know, it's a funny thing. Mario probably did a better job climbing than the others because he used all his wits. I'm not about to tell him he can't do what the other boys are doing."

Though it scares me now to think of climbing that building, all I remember feeling that day was the glorious flush of conquest and success. I felt alive. I am thankful that my Dad had the guts, and that's what it was, sheer guts, to let me be free and live my childhood fully. That summer day it thrilled me to know I had gone higher than ever before in my life. My parents had nothing but guts to rely on when it came to dealing with my blindness. They did not receive a proper diagnosis of what was causing my vision to fade until I was five years old.

When I was born in 1914, there was no cure or treatment even, for congenital glaucoma. Back then, Mom and Dad were on their own to figure out how to provide me the most normal childhood possible. They enlisted the help of my brother, Charlie. Charlie was three years older. He didn't want to be saddled with a whining, scared little brother, so he let me tag along wherever he went, whether it was just down the street to play, or to the top of four story skyscraper.

I followed my brother everywhere. He taught me to swim in the abandoned quarry (where swimming was strictly forbidden). On the days we felt especially adventurous, we got to the quarry by walking along the railroad trestle that spanned the White River. Before we started across, it was my job to place my ear upon the track to make sure there were no trains coming. As we walked across the trestle, I kept one hand resting on Charlie's shoulder. That way, I could match his steps and not step into the open air between the tracks. I could tell we were high above the water because the sounds of the river were muted. I said I followed Charlie everywhere, but that's not really true.

When it came time to enroll in the first grade, I could not follow Charlie and my friends from the neighborhood to school. None of the schools in my hometown of Muncie, Indiana, were prepared to teach a blind child. It was the first time in my life I really realized I was different from other kids. It was the first time my blindness had held me back from doing something I wanted to do.

My mother began to teach me basic reading and math skills at home, but she knew that was not a good long-term solution for my education. Over and over again Mom and Dad were told that I needed to be sent to the Indiana State School for the Blind in Indianapolis. Though I was terrified of leaving home, and my parents were just as scared to let me go, in the fall of 1922, when I was eight years old, I enrolled in the first grade at the state school for the blind.

The first few years at the school, I took the train home every weekend. My mother rode the train each Friday to pick me up at school and she rode back to Indianapolis with me early every Monday morning. She spent eight hours on the train each week.

A lot has changed at the state school since I was there. In the early 1920s the accommodations were utilitarian. I slept in a cold iron bed in a room with seven other boys until I graduated to rooms of just three in the fifth grade. There were separate dining halls for the girls and boys. In fact, boys and girls were kept apart at all times except for classes. In class the boys were seated on the left side of the room and girls to the right. We were not allowed to speak to one another or interact in any way. Of course, we all figured out ways to socialize with members of the opposite sex when we got older.

At the Indiana State School for the Blind, a whole new world opened up for me. I learned Braille and began to devour whatever literature I could get my hands on. I loved to use the topographical maps where I could feel the peaks of the tallest mountains and feel the breadth of the sea. Because there was no coddling at school, I learned to be completely independent. When I got older and more comfortable with my surroundings, my father made a deal with me. He said that times were tough financially, so he couldn't afford for me to ride the train home every weekend. If I agreed to stay at school for the weekend, he would put part of the cost of the train fare in a savings account for me. Well, I understood the value of a dollar, so I agreed.

As I began to spend weekends at school, I learned to travel into town. Most weekends, a group of us would go into town on Saturday for a Coke at Craig's Drug Store. What a treat. Though I became comfortable living at school, I relished my summers at home with Charlie.

One summer he taught me how to ride a bicycle. Once I learned to balance on the bike, Charlie rode beside me, talking to me all the way. By following the sound of his voice I could keep the bike in the road. When Charlie got his driving license in 1926, he taught me how to drive his old clunker. After he taught me how to accelerate, change gears, and stop the car, Charlie sat in the back seat with his hands on my shoulders. When he pressed on my right shoulder, I knew to turn right. We had a great time in those days. Not only did I relish the adventure and freedom Charlie helped me achieve, I absolutely reveled in the lavish attention he showered upon me. Somehow, during those memorable summers, no harm came to me or Charlie. Our escapades built my confidence, so my independence continued to grow.

After graduation from high school, I enrolled in the same undergraduate program at Ball State that Charlie had completed. He was working on his law degree at Notre Dame by then, but we had big plans of practicing law together some day. I lived at home while I attended Ball State and had no trouble mastering the layout of the campus. Fellow students served as my readers and I graduated from Ball State with relative ease.

That was not the case at Notre Dame. No blind person had ever attended the law school at Notre Dame, so the administration and teaching staff were not quite sure what to do with me Nor were my fellow students. Once again, I became painfully aware that I was different from everyone else. Worst of all, I was terribly lonely. Weekends were the hardest. While the students were nice enough when they saw me on campus, no one invited me to their dorm room for a beer. No one invited me to any parties or to the picture show. I began to question whether I was good enough, smart enough, to make it at Notre

Dame.

It was the first time I had questioned my ability to succeed. Though I knew the first year of law school was going to be rigorous, designed to weed out a large percentage of the class, I was not prepared for the amount of reading that was required. I chose several students to read the textbooks to me, but it was virtually impossible to accomplish all of the reading that was assigned each night. As my student readers labored through tedious chapters, I took copious notes in Braille. There was so much material to study every night that my calloused fingertips became numb and the tiny dots of Braille began to wear off the paper.

Dear God, I cannot do this, I thought night after night. My fingers flew over page after page of Braille, but I never felt I had studied enough. Many of the intricate legal concepts were always just beyond my reach. The first semester I was filled with an almost crippling sense of panic. The panic was far worse than my lack of sight. I became convinced that I would not make it through the semester, much less the year.

Everyone knew the first year of law school was the weed-out year. A large portion of the class would fail their courses and not be back the following year. When I received my grades for the first semester, I was shocked that I had passed. However, my passing grades did little to bolster my confidence. Second semester loomed ahead of me. It was supposed to be even tougher. I was perpetually exhausted and my sense of panic did not dissipate.

Throughout that first year of law school, I kept thinking about my future. If I could not make it through law school and pass the bar, what would happen to me? Other students who didn't make it through had all sorts of other business and teaching options. Not me. What other skills did I possess? The worst part of it all was that I had no one to talk to. I was so scared, but I was terrified that if I verbalized my fears they would surely come to pass. I could not share my burden with my mother because it would be too difficult for her to bear. So I lived with my angst alone. It was the loneliest time of my life.

That first year, I often found myself longing for the carefree summer days when Charlie and I played tag and roamed our neighborhood until the sun went down. Those days were a lifetime away. They were from a time in my life where there was no fear of failure, just bold, joyous living. Though I feared I would, I didn't fail my courses at Notre Dame. I managed to graduate in 1940 with honors. Now only the bar exam loomed between me and the desk Charlie had waiting for me at his law office. The problem was that no blind person had ever taken the Indiana State Bar, so I was unsure how the exam would be administered.

I was taken aback when the Board of Examiners told me they had decided to give me the test orally. All I could think was that it was one thing to fail an exam privately, through the written word. It was quite another to fall on your face in front of the entire Board of Examiners.

Once the questioning began, the knots in my stomach began to relax. I knew the material and was able to articulate my answers clearly. Though I did not receive the official results of my exam for several weeks, by letting me know what the correct answers were to the exam, the board let me know I had passed. What a feeling of accomplishment that was. Now I could practice law with Charlie. My life has been full. Not only did I practice law for many years, but I also served two terms as a Superior Court Judge of Indiana.

However, the greatest gift in my life was my marriage to a wonderful woman I met at the State School For The Blind. Jane lost her vision to congenital glaucoma in the fourth grade. She and I enjoyed almost fifty-eight years of marriage before Jane passed away. We raised four sighted children who mean the world to me today. Jane and I were able to achieve a level of independence few people though possible, or even wise. We owned our own homes and got along with less help than most of our sighted friends. Jane and I were the only two from our high school graduating class who went on to college.

I don't know what made us different. Maybe it was the expectations we had for ourselves and our desire to be independent, like other people. Maybe it was the expectations other people, like Charlie, had for us. Maybe it was that we never thought of ourselves as handicapped. I don't know what made the difference.

What I do know is that when I look back over the years of my life, I am satisfied. I have enjoyed a good life thanks to my loving family, a happy marriage, and many friends along the way. Now I am a lucky old man with happy memories and not too many regrets.

Susan Stall worked as an assistant for Mario Pieroni and his wife for two years during her undergraduate work at UNC Chapel Hill. Mrs. Stall, her husband, and two young sons live in Greenville, South Carolina.

My Son the Actor
Margaret Kramar

Every mother knows the feeling. On every painted cardboard tree at every school play hang the hearts of anxious mothers whose child, peering out from an oversized dragon costume, is much more beautiful and talented than all the rest. Now parents filled the wooden bleachers in the elementary school gymnasium, buzzing with anticipation before the talent show was to begin. The performing children were seated to the left of the bare stage, waiting for the black baby grand piano to come alive under their fingers, and the lone, skinny microphone to resonate with their voices.

I could see Spenser with the straw cowboy hat and cord dangling under his chin, wearing his jeans and borrowed cowboy boots. Where was that Western shirt we had found for him? Why was he wearing the t-shirt with frogs that he had worn to school that day? I may have been perturbed about the shirt, but nothing detracted from Spenser's confidence. His platinum blond hair peeped out from under the brim of his hat, and he surveyed the restless audience with a bright, knowing smile. It was going to be his day on stage, dressed as Woody, singing "When Somebody Loved Me."

I fingered the camcorder nervously, checking to make sure the screen lit up. I told myself that of course Spenser would be fine, but underneath the drone of the audience, I reminded myself that after all he was not a normal child, and that the unexpected is always ready to eclipse any happy moment.

"Mrs. Thomas, may I have a short word with you outside?"

The voice of the school principal interrupted my thoughts, and I searched his ruddy, jocular face for a clue. This was the same principal who played monsters with Spenser on the playground, who had told Spenser after seeing his act, "Why, Spenser, I had no idea I was in the presence of a famous actor. You're really a star!" This principal loved the school and led brilliantly, always the optimist. I could smell the floral perfume of other mothers who were crowding the doorway as I followed him into the hall. Now what had happened? What was this wonderful man being asked to do?

Once outside in the shiny hall of gleaming linoleum, I could see a tinge of disappointment hiding just behind the steely gray brightness of his eyes.

"We've just had a phone call from your husband. He states that as Spenser's father he is forbidding Spenser to participate in this talent show, and as you can imagine, that puts the school in an awkward position."

"Why, what is his reasoning?" I asked, always the one to tilt at windmills.

"Well, I guess for him there's the issue of Spenser's disability. The secretary took the phone call initially but when he talked to me he was expressing something about Spenser being an embarrassment or failure, or. . . I guess what we need to do now is make some kind of decision about this."

He looked at me and waited. I wanted to be swallowed up by the shiny linoleum floor, be sucked down to some magical paradise where things could go right for once, where Spenser was a typically developing child, and the eternal battle over this finally ended.

I thought back to the day he was born, and my initial gut reaction upon first seeing him: is that the baby?

I would always feel guilty that this was my first impression after I surfaced from the anesthesia of childbirth, but with his little wizened elongated face and slightly slanted eyes, he did look strange.

The doctors and nurses who surrounded him viewed him from one angle and then another. No, they decided, this was not a happy outcome, and they rolled the isolette bearing his little body into the neonatal intensive care unit, where gleaming plaques memorialize babies who have died.

The pediatrician, whom I knew from high school as a scrawny kid with a beautiful tenor voice, looked somberly down at the baby.

"Sam, Sam," I implored, "just tell me that he's eventually going to be all right."

He stared down at the baby. Since high school his frame had filled out and his hair no longer stood out in unruly tufts.

"I can't promise you that because I don't know, Susan," was his reply.

I rushed back to my hospital room, and surveyed through tears the baby gifts lining the counters and window sills. They came from well-wishing friends and relatives, who only wondered whose eyes and hair he had. Now the blue, green and pink pastels of the crocheted blanket bled together in jeering hues. The corpulent teddy bear, who knew but would not tell, stared blankly through his wire glasses, joining the conspiracy formed by the spotted giraffe and fluffy lion. Only a macabre choo-choo train engine, with an insolent cap perched upon his head, dared to break the silence with a mocking rendition of "Happy Days Are Here Again."

Every day in the hospital, the woman from the department of vital statistics came to find me staring blankly at the wall. She wanted a name for the birth certificate, but my husband and I couldn't agree: couldn't agree that this happened, couldn't agree on how it would change our lives, couldn't agree on what to name a broken dream. But one night I wandered into the neonatal intensive care unit and perched before his isolette. He looked so strange and forsaken as he lay there alone, yet despite all the sadness, he was my child. I would hold him. He was so light and so long, as he rested in the folds of my yellow-paper sterile gown. I looked down at him, and bent over to kiss his forehead.

"Hello, you," I whispered to him. I knew then that I was going to love him despite the rest of the world, and that his name would be Spenser.

Suddenly Spenser lit up like a Christmas tree. His previously expressionless face glowed all at once with a smile that stretched from ear to ear. This smile was to be the first of many surprises.

The official diagnosis was Sotos Syndrome. It is estimated to occur once in every 10,000 births, and possibly results from an autosomal dominant inheritance pattern. Affected children are characterized by advanced bone age, advanced growth in early childhood, an antimongoloid slant of the eyelids, a pointed chin or moderate prognathism, a large, dolichocephalic head and prominent forehead, poor motor coordination and verbal and motor delays. Do with it what you will.

When he was two months old, Spenser, his dad and I were in another hospital waiting room. I looked down at Spenser in his infant seat, wrapped in a blue crocheted afghan, his eyes tightly shut. He was motionless, almost catatonic, somewhat in that liminal zone where souls hover between life and death. Worry shrouded the gray padding surrounding his head, and fear beamed down from the fluorescent lights onto the upholstered chairs, lined neatly in institutional style. A father played with his toddlers with red and yellow plastic legos a thousand miles away. Nothing could rip away the membranes that enveloped his dad and I in our grief. It sat beside me as I put on my makeup in the morning, it bleeped its sad tidings from the microwave oven at dinnertime, and put up a barrier between us in our bed at night. We each laid ourselves out in our separate catacombs since the birth, not touching each other.

A hospital technician escorted us to a room where an occupational therapist would assess Spenser's developmental progress. I laid him on his back where plush blocks and a rolling ball were within his grasp. Spenser lay there very still, not seeing or touching them.

"That baby is not going to play with those toys," Spenser's dad commented to the physical therapist.

"But you have to understand that he had a very difficult birth, and that's going to set him back. It's the same with preemies, and they eventually catch up," I chimed in.

His dad remained sullen and the therapist put on her happy face reserved for interacting with babies. She held things in front of him, tried to roll him over, and proceeded through a battery of tests. Spenser failed everything. The leaden silence shouted that his dad was right, and I gathered up my diaper bag, blankets, and hospital forms along with Spenser and my battered optimism, and schlepped out of there as quickly and efficiently as I could.

Later that night his dad and I bustled around in the kitchen, heating things up in the microwave. He still wore his coat and tie from work, and paused with his hand resting on the oven door.

"Susan, I'm seeing a therapist and he's put me on some medication. I'm having terrible headaches and feeling very anxious and tense all the time. I just can't take it anymore."

"Well, of course. Anything that helps," I answered. Then as usual he went to bed early, and for me into the wee hours of the morning there was prayer, journaling, reading, trying to see a glimmer of hope. Anything that helps.

Spenser was far behind at the four-month evaluation, and things were no better at six months. Then due to untreated esophagitis, he became a virtual skeleton. When springtime flowers were bursting forth and it was time to dress him in summer baby clothes, he was no more than skin and bones. It's a miracle that he didn't die.

The weather got warmer still and soon it was the end of May. The wind whooshed behind me, slamming the door prematurely as I arrived home from work. I immediately sensed that there was something different about the house. In the living room, there was a huge bare spot where the red velvet couch had been. In the kitchen, there was no dining room table in the corner. I opened the door of the blue hutch and thumbed through the checkbook registry. All the money had been withdrawn except for about one hundred dollars.

"You'll need to call the telephone company and put the service in your name by Tuesday," I turned to face Spenser's dad, "otherwise they'll cut it off." I studied him standing there, as serious as he had ever been. That was the last thing he said to me. Then he turned, went down the stairs, and walked out of the house and our lives.

That same weekend the neighbors had a huge party. Cars lined our driveway and the street, and people mingled in the green grass with beer, food and laughter. A rock band was stationed in their garage, and the pulsating rhythms of the bass permeated our bedroom windows. The sounds of the conversation and the music wouldn't leave us alone, and called us out into the intoxicating night air. Still numbed by shock, I gathered up Spenser and went next door, into the heart of the dance. Life was calling to us, teasing and cajoling us. It just wouldn't take "no" for an answer.

Before Spenser was born, I had been quite the actress in local theatre productions. I loved, it, loved it, loved it, even if another actor doused my character with cold water, and I stood shivering in the wings, with a smelly, damp raincoat and droopy hat. I loved being behind the footlights, knowing that the audience probably doesn't notice the saliva from the actors' mouths as it sprays in an arc through the air, launched by precise articulation. The many blurred faces morph into a huge sleeping beast that grunts and grumbles, sometimes roused by the cackling electricity of pandemic laughter. You shout, squeal or cry into this crowded darkness, and the audience always echoes back. There's no other dialogue quite like it, and once smitten, you never forget.

Now as for Spenser, he caught a wave and kept sailing on with his life. The gloomy prognoses forecast at the time of his birth never materialized. He did walk and talk, albeit several months behind schedule, but he eventually did everything, his way. Then he smiled, danced to music, shattered a bowl on the floor, ate spaghetti, and all the dark hair he was born with was replaced by a silvery golden blonde. Nobody looked twice at this child in McDonald's except to smile back and wave. We must not have told him about the dire predictions, the dark clouds surrounding his birth, or maybe he just wasn't listening. He was too busy going platinum. By the time he was about eight, this little boy was tall and thin, and had a habit of sometimes cocking his head to one side if there was something he didn't quite understand. When he smiled, a dimple caved in part of his cheek. He was up for anything, and this little boy loved being on stage.

"Let's go into my office where we can discuss this privately, Mrs. Thomas," said the principal. He sat across from me at his desk, sleeves rolled up and hands clenched together. He leaned forward, ready to speak, just as his secretary edged into the room after a slight pause.

"The superintendent is on the line with the district test results. He really wants to talk to you before he leaves for the conference," she said.

Slightly rolling his eyes, he left the room, with an apology. I looked around at the walls. A trophy, a banner, a picture of an awards assembly in the auditorium from years ago. Gazing into the proscenium, I remembered a Friday night when Spenser was five. The fledgling thespians were to showcase their talents, and I found a seat in one of many darkened auditoriums, climbing over mothers, grandparents, cousins and little brothers and sisters who wriggled and jumped, arms and legs shooting in every direction. The audience quieted.

Suddenly Spenser's group filed onto the stage. There was Spenser, beaming, glowing, lit up. The footlights and overhead spots seemed much brighter. His face was completely illuminated, and he smiled broadly. Because he was taller, he was in the back row, but he did not stay there. Before the song began, he gently pushed his way into the front row, and the children quietly parted to let him in. Then Spenser was front and center. Perhaps it was the light reflecting from his platinum blond hair, or because my heart leapt through to him past the darkness, but I was mesmerized. I could not take my eyes off him. Surely everyone in the audience was focused on this bright, happy child, glowing with confidence, on the same ray as the music, being beamed to the stars. All the other children were so gray. Were they there at all?

Their number was over, so the children started walking off, first the front row, then the back. Spenser remained, standing erect, still beaming a bright smile. He drank in the audience and would not leave, fixed to the spot. The next group of children emerged from the wings and started taking their places. Still Spenser would not leave. Finally a woman emerged from behind the side curtain to escort him off, and the audience murmured a muffled laughter, but something of him remained. I had never known him to be so happy.

Another memory, Spenser backstage congratulating his peers who performed in a local production of Peter Pan, and a young cast member approached him with "Spenser, Spenser! Hey everybody, Spenser's here!" More children came out, as if magically summoned. They regarded Spenser with delight, as though he contained all the wonder of the Neverland they reveled in onstage. Nobody had ever made such a fuss over me, ever.

From the principal's office, I could imagine the excitement Spenser must now be feeling, sitting on the bleachers, eagerly awaiting a chance to show off his stuff. He believed in himself, and he didn't care if anyone else did, just like that time in Washington, D.C., when he was dancing on the subway. Yes, dancing on the subway. We were all sitting there, and he slowly got up, went to the middle of the aisle, and started dancing in a slow, syncopated rhythm. He smiled broadly and his dancing became more energized. A tired old woman wearing a cloth coat looked the other way, but the Hispanic with jet black hair glanced at him and smiled. So did the girl with a pierced eyebrow and green hair. They knew, Spenser and the rest, and the beat pulsed through their veins. It was life, life in the gray dullness of that city subway, coming to get them, whirling them around, never letting them go. Why couldn't his father understand this?

"Sorry for the interruption," said the principal. I focused on the orderliness of the pinstripes in his shirt before the solution boiled to the surface and words started tumbling out of my mouth.

"I'll deal with it," I blurted out to the principal. "Whether he writes out a formal complaint, or files a lawsuit or whatever, send all the correspondence to me. The school will be totally off the hook. It's our problem, not yours. I promise you, somehow I'll deal with him."

The principal stood there in the balance between being the responsible administrator and the overgrown little boy who still loved to pretend that he was a monster on the playground.

"Well, maybe we'll just tell him that it was too late to stop the performance," he said with a twinkle in his eye.

As applause in the auditorium subsided, I heard the mistress of ceremonies announce the next act: Spenser. Clutching my camcorder, I found a seat in time to watch my son the actor, sailing onto the stage with a smile.

Margaret Rayburn Kramar teaches freshman composition at the University of Kansas where she is earning a Ph.D. degree in literature. She and her family live in Big Springs, Kansas, where they grow organic vegetables and free-range chickens.

The Learning Disabled Daughter Turns Thirty
Juditha Dowd

The grace that eluded you quickens tonight
as you round second base and pound toward third,
your stride lengthened by some late-blooming angel.

You don't hear me and I'm glad—Run! I'm shrieking,
bring it home! and because this is Florida,
where night leagues and church teams are big-time,
I'm not alone—
Everyone is yelling what the runner ought to do.

You can't hear me and I'm glad because you're right
to slide, grinning, into third and hang there.
The sidelong glance from a work-weathered dad
next to me in the bleachers says Lady,
don't you know anything about baseball?

I do. I know about baseball. And basketball.
I know your nose broken by someone else's cartwheel,
the endless races where you tore in, spent and red-faced,
last. And theory, and experts and time.

Tonight it's as if the thief repents,
returns your heirloom silver with a note:
It's all here. . .except the spoons I melted down.
Sorry, hope you didn't need them.

Here in the dusty diamond, the fading light
you have every tool you need.
You've outrun the taunts of classmates,

the grades, the accolades you never got,
those driver's tests you studied for and failed.

What is it? you cried as I drove you home
after your fourth, but not your final try.
What the hell is wrong with me?

Tonight I can answer Nothing,
nothing in the least
Take up your fork again, my girl
and join the feast.

Primarily a poet, Juditha Dowd also writes fiction and creative nonfiction. Her work has appeared in many print and online journals. Her chapbook, The Weathermancer, which contains this poem, is just out from Finishing Line Press. The mother of five daughters, she lives in western New Jersey with her husband, James.

Lagging Behind My Father
John Lee Clark

I lingered on the hill
where my father often walked
as a boy, perhaps daydreaming

just like I was, eyes
deep in their sockets
so not to see too much.

Then my eyes peered out
of their sweet recess
to see the sidewalk ahead

no longer carrying my father.
So I ran, my feet pounding
the sloping squares

of muted light bridging
over the swell of land
that suddenly became air.

My surprised legs floundered
then wheeled mysteriously
as I swam through sky,

somersaulting once, again,
my fingers brushing
concrete as a heel bumped

against the railing
of the stairs leading down
to where my father stood waiting.

His mouth opened
as I somehow landed,
staggering but still standing

as his first son, eyes
slowly peering out again
after a dream just lived.

John Lee Clark is a second-generation deaf-blind man living in St. Paul, Minnesota. His writings have appeared in many publications, among them Ache, The Deaf-Blind American, McSweeney's, *and* Poetry. *The recipient of The Robert F. Panara Award for Poetry from the National Association of the Deaf and grants from VSA Arts of Minnesota, Jerome Foundation, and Minnesota State Arts Board, Clark was honored as a featured artist at the Deaf Way II International Cultural Arts Festival. A poem of his was also selected as the Best Sports Poem of 2005 by Kent State University's* The Listening Eye *and another poem was selected for the "Poem of the Day" program on Martha Stewart Radio Satellite. Aside from pursuing a self-designed degree in Deaf-Blind Studies at Metropolitan State University, Clark enjoys canoeing, tandem bicycling, cooking, and knitting.*

Claire's First Song
Barbara Neal Varma

"She's what?" the professor asked in surprise as if he were the one who couldn't hear.

"She's deaf," I said again, and then quickly added, "and I'm her interpreter."

The professor's stare remained on us despite the explanation. I couldn't fault his reaction; after all, I had made this announcement while standing in his Beginning Piano class.

My client, Claire, fidgeted from behind her front-row piano keyboard, no doubt eager to know what her instructor was saying. He cast a wary glance her way as if he doubted her inability to overhear his concern then looked at me again. "But this is a piano class." His pale blue eyes squinted in confusion. "If she can't hear, how can she learn to play?"

How indeed? Truth was, I'd been wondering the same thing myself but didn't reply. Instead, I turned to face Claire and signed, "YOU DEAF. CAN'T HEAR PIANO. HOW YOU LEARN?" I used not only my hands, but my face, the movement of my mouth, even how I held my body, slightly hunched over like the professor.

Registering comprehension now, Claire smiled at her teacher and signed: "ME REGISTER FOR CLASS. PIANO."

"I've registered for this class," I said.

"PIANO."

"Piano."

"THAT MY INTERPRETER."

"That's my interpreter."

"SHE INTERPRET FOR ME."

"She'll translate everything for me."

The professor's head turned from side to side, unsure of which one of us to look at: his signing student or me speaking a language he could hear and understand.

Claire dropped her hands, calmly waiting for him to take up his turn in the conversation. If she understood the inherent complexity of having a deaf student in a music class she gave no clue, continuing to regard her new instructor with steady expectation. He returned the favor. Then he quickly turned and retreated to the front of the class, apparently deciding to pursue this puzzle at another time.

I breathed a sigh of relief and gave Claire a quick, reassuring smile before walking over to retrieve a chair from the corner of the classroom. As was customary for Sign Language interpreters, I positioned myself up front and to the left of the instructor, facing my client. The better for me to hear; the better for the client to see. The professor stood quietly behind his podium. I could still feel the heat of his attention but he made no objection and didn't challenge me. I sat without further incident.

This was the beginning of a new semester at the community college but it was not the first time I had interpreted for Claire. She was in year eight of what should have been a two-year degree program, but Claire's academic path had other considerations not imposed upon the "typical" community college student. First, of course, was her disability, which slowed down the communication process. Her pace was further dictated by her husband, the designated leader of her traditional Greek family, who advised her to take "just one class" per semester to not interfere with her duties at home.

The professor adjusted the position of his podium, occasionally looking up to survey his small kingdom of a classroom. His young subjects were seated behind four neat rows of electronic pianos and music stands. Fluorescent ceiling lights focused on the students and their instruments, casting a sheen to both. The musty scent of textbooks and tennis shoes still lingered in the room.

The professor tapped the podium's wooden edge with his baton, staring down his audience until they were still.

"This is Beginning Piano," he said with authority and then launched into what seemed to be a well-used speech. As I interpreted for Claire, the professor sent a few nervous glances our way but for the most part ignored our commotion.

Behind her keyboard, Claire sat perfectly still. She looked young for a woman with two children, her youthful appearance accentuated by round wire-rimmed glasses. It was easy to see she was excited about the class; hazel eyes drank in every sign, every expression, eager to understand the professor's words. When he instructed the students to "Play a C chord," Claire placed her hands gently on the keys, ready to begin.

"Begin," said the professor with a downward wave of his baton.

"BEGIN," I signed.

A variety of sounds suddenly filled the room, some of which I recognized as a C chord, others not. Claire's was in the latter category, but being unable to hear her mistake she made no attempt to correct it and continued to hold the discordant chord with confidence. The professor heard the off chime and looked around for its source, tilting his head to guide him to the sour note. He approached Claire and bent down to correctly place her hands, then strode back to his place in front of the class—but not before directing a telling gaze my way: This isn't going to work.

He raised his baton to cue a second attempt. Challenged now, I quickly gained Claire's attention and signed "AGAIN," my right hand moving up and over in a half-circle arc to land in the waiting palm of my left hand. I breathed a sigh of relief when she got it this time and won the chance to continue.

We went to class twice a week; Claire always eager, the professor always wary. The musical ingredient was the obvious wrench in the works. Every class, I tried a different interpreting technique to better—and more quickly—convey the message. No doubt the normal lag time associated with interpreting from one language to another was made more pronounced by the addition of music. As the class progressed from notes to chords, phrases to songs, Claire's contribution was always a beat behind. The class would begin…and then Claire. The song would end…and then Claire. The giggles from her hearing classmates, not to mention a few copycats adding their own trailing notes, only fueled the professor's growing disapproval.

Her first exam didn't go well. In a room with just Claire and me, the professor and a piano, her mid-term attempt was classically imperfect. The professor looked slightly smug behind his normal reserve. I was disappointed—more so than I'd been hired to be. As an interpreter I've been conditioned to be the anonymous third party, present to communicate, not to intervene or even want to. But as I heard the discordant chords crying from the keyboard I realized I was as committed as Claire. I'd been chosen for the assignment because I could also play piano; my supervisor felt my insider's knowledge would help to bridge the gap for this unusual situation, but with this blatant failure at first attempt I knew I needed to do more.

I obtained permission from my supervisor to also tutor Claire and made an unscheduled appearance at her next practice session. We met at one of the small rooms next to the main classroom, each one containing an upright piano and only enough space to encourage attention. She was pleased but puzzled to see me. I explained I was now assigned to coach as well as interpret her lessons, but first I needed to know something.

"Claire," I signed, using my fingers to spell her name. "Why do you want to play the piano?"

She blushed a little. "My family loves music." She signed "family" with emphasis, telling me how important it was for her to feel included among her otherwise hearing family.

She went on to describe the various instruments she'd seen her family play. Her husband played the guitar, her sister the flute and her young daughter the violin. Then her eyes shone even more brightly as she paraded her fingers up and down an imaginary keyboard, swaying her body side to side for added effect.

"Who plays the piano?" I asked.

"No one," she signed. "But I've seen others play and I think it's very pretty."

I'd never thought of that. "Do you have a piano?"

"Oh yes. It's from my sister. I want the kids to learn."

I still wasn't convinced. "But Claire, how will you do it? I mean, you can't hear the notes…"

Claire became very serious, her chin rising in a stubborn pose. "I just want to play one song, a Christmas song, that's all. I know I can do it and then I'll play it for my family at Christmas. It will be pretty," her hands insisted.

We stood for a moment regarding each other.

"Okay," I agreed. "We can learn a song. I know how to play the piano and could help you practice if you like." Claire eagerly nodded, the universal signs for YES.

I first explained the inner workings of the keyboard; something the professor didn't need to do with his hearing students. We lifted the lid on the upright and peered into the dim interior filled with tightly wound strings and soft pads that moved at the strike of a key.

"The pad hits the string," I signed. "It's like a bell; it makes a sound."

She looked confused so I brought her attention back to the sheet music propped on the mantel. "See that C note?"

She nodded, blushing again as she remembered the professor's correction of her hands. I pressed the key. She leaned over the top to watch the pad move and tap the string. She looked at me expectantly. I nodded and pointed towards my ear.

She looked again to study the long parade of strings and then back at me. "Why are there so many?"

"They all have different sounds." I searched my mental library of signs to think of a visual match. "The higher notes," I ventured, gesturing to the keys on the right side of the keyboard, "the 'happier' the sound." I hoped my "happy" expression was convincing. "The lower notes have a deeper sound. When you play the music," I said, pointing to her sheet music and the jumping array of notes on the page, "the sounds are different and we hear..." I finished the sentence by moving my hands up and down and away from each other, dancing in the air. She slowly nodded, still not quite understanding, but willing to accept the explanation for the moment.

That little discussion took almost all of our lesson time and much of my imagination, interpreting or otherwise, but I was confident in our beginning.

I pointed to my watch. "Time's up. We'll do this again on Thursday."

Many Tuesdays and Thursdays followed. Outside the leaves changed their tune from green to gold to copper brown; inside I tried to paint the picture of music for Claire.

For timing, I sat on the bench beside her and gently tapped my foot to hers, serving as a human metronome as I signaled the rhythm of the music. The strange italicized words on the page were a mystery to her so we increased her vocabulary. "Presto" meant "PLAY-PIANO FAST." "Andante" meant "PLAY-PIANO SLOW." "Pianissimo" meant "PLAY-PIANO GENTLE."

I taught her to memorize the songs, just as her eyes had memorized signs when she was young. A deaf child knows when her name is being "called," sees the shape of it on her mother's hand even before she learns the fingerspelled letters. So for Claire I guided her hands to memorize the shape of the music. It had to "feel" right, because sound was going to be of no benefit for us.

Repetition was our religion. I lost count of how many times I signed "AGAIN," my right hand memorizing its own path as it moved up and over in a small arc to meet my left hand's waiting palm. When she hit a wrong note I tapped her shoulder, alerting her to the error that could not be heard. She would then begin again at the measure before and continue through until either I interrupted her or she completed the verse. As the semester wore on she completed the verse more often.

She chose a Christmas carol, ironically "Silent Night" to be her one and only performance for both family and professor. We practiced it often until I heard the famous tune continually—though she, of course, was spared the mental reruns.

One noteworthy error, easily corrected, happened one afternoon when Claire proceeded to practice her lesson only in the range above middle C. I asked her why, preferring to hear the reason before attempting a correction. She grinned. "I want to play only happy notes." I nodded, remembering my "happy notes' version of music theory. I eventually convinced her that all the notes were equally important and from then on I avoided emotional equivalents to sound descriptions, letting the visual examples carry the message.

In class Claire's improvement was evident but still behind her peers' musical achievements. Hers was still the remaining note—but now it was the right one and the other students had thankfully lost interest for performing in the round.

The professor rarely came around to us now. In the beginning he had occasionally approached Claire, using frustrated and hurried motions to correct her errors, even standing next to her keyboard waving his baton to impress a notion of timing. But after a few weeks of apparent failure to fix the problem he stopped acknowledging her altogether; practicing the child's remedy of making something bad disappear by simply ignoring it. Claire's excitement never varied despite the declining stages of his instruction. She remained consistent with her attendance and effort, if not her musical accuracy.

One time he did express a moment's interest. "Could she ever hear?" he asked me. I interpreted the question for Claire who shook her head "NO" and went on to explain that her mother had contracted rheumatic fever during pregnancy. Hearing tests done when Claire was a still a toddler discovered that deafness was the reason for her inattentive behavior. But the professor had stopped listening after she'd signed, "NO," dejectedly heading back to the safety of his podium. When Claire saw his interest had been only fleeting she returned her hands to the keys and awaited his next instruction, determined to simply keep going with or without him.

The final exam landed on a chill winter's day under an otherwise sunny sky. Winter coats were dusted off from their summer captivity and donned in eagerness of the arriving Christmas holiday. Claire and I already knew the required testing arena and the strict rules that were meant to impose fairness and objectivity. She would be on her own. I was allowed to be there only as her interpreter, leaving my tutoring hat at home.

Claire arrived on time, her hair slightly mussed from the winter wind. She removed her coat to reveal a modest green velvet dress with white collar and sleeves. She greeted the professor with her usual quiet smile and then paused expectantly, waiting to be told to take her seat and begin.

The professor gestured toward the piano with a slight bow, seeming intent on extending the dignity of the situation despite his misgivings. Looking at me he asked, "What song shall she play?"

I knew the answer, of course, but resisted answering for Claire, and signed the question to her.

She nodded and signed, "SILENT NIGHT," her hands making a graceful path in the air. The professor's hands rose and for a moment I thought he was going to try the signs on, just to see how they played, but then he changed his mind and sent his hands deep into his pockets instead.

"Fine," he said and nodded, waiting for her to begin. I returned to my place a pace back from Claire while she took her seat at the piano. The sudden quiet in the room, so normal for Claire, added to my nervousness, but she seemed calm as her fingers found the keys they'd practiced to remember.

She began, and the familiar tune of "Silent Night" filled the small room.

I wish she could have heard it. It was perfect. Each note a confirmation of her desire to do something they told her she couldn't do. Though no words accompanied the notes, my mind filled in the missing lyrics just as her hands filled in the silence. "Silent night, Holy night. All is calm, all is bright…"

Finally the last ringing tone faded away, the effect guided by a slow release of her hands from the keys, foot from the pedal.

She turned towards me, a questioning expression on her face. I smiled and nodded, but only slightly, not wanting to delay her gaze from the professor. He was staring at her in amazement.

"Why…that's incredible!" He looked at me and repeated, "That's incredible!"

And then back to Claire. "My dear, that was excellent. I wouldn't have believed it…" His voice faded away as smoothly as her final note. Then he brightened and turned towards me. "I wonder…could she play it for me again?"

He studied my hands as they signed "AGAIN" and then turned back to Claire. Awkwardly his right hand moved up and over in a small half-circle arc to land in the middle of his left palm. "AGAIN." The professor's first sign.

She beamed, and turned back to the piano to repeat her song.

As "Silent Night" once again filled the room I quietly surveyed the scene: Claire, the piano, and the professor. All is calm…all is bright….

Claire was right, I decided. It really was very pretty.

Barbara Neal Varma is a freelance writer and Sign Language interpreter. Her essays have won awards from Writer's Digest *magazine, the National Writers Association, and* Anthology *magazine. Barbara is currently working on* Interpreting Life, *a memoir of inspirational true stories including "Claire's First Song."*

The Bravest Sister of All
Judith Stevens

It was in the late '40s, early '50s when a monster intruded upon our childhood.

The name of the monster was poliomyelitis, also known as infantile paralysis or simply, polio. A polio epidemic was sweeping the country, leaving scores of children in iron lungs or with weakened, atrophied limbs in its wake.

One day it visited our house.

My sister, Jeanette, and I were two years apart in age. I idolized her and much to her annoyance, followed her everywhere, like a faithful puppy. She was eight years old and in the third grade; I was six.

Jeanette and I shared a breezy bedroom in the old house that belonged to my grandmother. It sat on a corner at the top of a hill in a sleepy Southern town.

We lived there with our parents, two brothers and a smaller sister, and for a time, our aunt and uncle, in an extended family setting that was quite common during those days. Along with the other neighborhood children, we played in our large backyard, skated, rode our bicycles, and after a rain, waded together in the muddy water that cascaded down the hill, filling the gutters with the gurgling sound of a small river, as it raced to the waiting water main, just around the corner.

Not once did we imagine that within the brown rushing water lurked a virus that was capable of producing paralysis of certain muscle groups or of entire organs or limbs. We never dreamed that a tiny unseen enemy might enter our bodies through something as innocent as a small cut or scratch on a child's foot and inflame the grey matter of the spinal cord, altering, or in some instances, silencing a life forever.

It was shortly after a spring rain on an unusually warm day that we joined our friends, cavorting barefoot in the dirty water, that something unusual happened to my sister, Jeanette. The next day when we went to school, she was playing "Swinging Statues" in the schoolyard. Without warning, she fell down.

No one pushed her; in fact, no one touched her. Her legs simply gave way.

This astonished her, but she got up and went inside the school building, putting it out of her mind. She never mentioned it to my parents.

In the next day or so, Jeanette developed the classic sudden symptoms of polio: fever, headache, sore throat, stiff neck, gastrointestinal complaints, and pain in her back and limbs. My grandmother kept her home and I walked to school alone, uneasy and worried.

The next morning when I awoke, Jeanette was trying to get out of bed.

"Help me," she said. "My legs won't work."

I called my four-year-old brother, Bill, and each of us took one of her arms under the shoulders, but she was too heavy for us to handle.

"I'll get Daddy," I shouted, racing away like the wind on spindly legs.

For the rest of my life, I will remember my slightly built father, leaning over our bed with infinite tenderness, gently lifting my sister and carrying her to the bathroom. I waited outside the door, puzzled, anxious, and hoping against hope, that the grownups would know what to do to fix Jeanette's legs so that she would be able to walk again.

Our doctor came to the house and made his dreadful diagnosis. After that, a procession of doctors, specialists, reporters and official looking people with badges and equipment came and went. It seemed as if the entire Petersburg Health Department had descended upon 530 Wythe Street and life, as we had known it, ended. Once the official diagnosis was made, Jeanette was loaded into an ambulance and whisked away from us to a research hospital in nearby Richmond—the Medical College of Virginia.

As for the rest of us, we were quarantined. All four remaining children and our friends had to be poked, prodded and tested, not once, but several times, to determine that we did not have the polio virus, too. The doctors whispered that it was a miracle. That highly contagious disease had claimed only one victim - the eldest of five children living in close proximity. Of all our neighborhood friends who had waded with us in the deadly water, only one child contracted polio: my sister. Jeanette had become a statistic in the mounting polio epidemic and our lives were changed forever.

I clung to the inner connection that kept Jeanette close to me, writing her poems, stories, and spending countless hours making little gifts to send to her via my aunt, grandmother and parents. (In those days, children under twelve were not allowed in hospitals, so I was unable to visit her. I felt as if a part of my body had been ripped away, leaving a wound that I revisited again and again.) I decorated little plastic trees, hanging her favorite gum-drops on the branches, to distract her for a moment from the disease, and sent books of her favorite

Lifesaver candies to tempt her and bring a smile.

Meanwhile, the grownups tiptoed around, occasionally whispering foreign sounding words—new terms to decipher—that seized me with new fear: "polio," "paralyzed," and the dreaded "iron lung" (which produced visions of torture devices). No doubt in the belief that we were "too young to understand what was going on," I was left to piece together my own truth of what was happening.

In addition to the letters, gifts and cards, I responded by sending the same urgent mental affirmation, thought and prayer over and over and over again to my sister:

"Walk, Jeanette, WALK."

My brave sister endured the painful therapies of the day that seem archaic when examined in these times. She was first confined to an iron lung—a huge metal respirator that induces breathing in a patient whose respiratory muscles are paralyzed. For a small girl with a fear of tiny spaces and confinement, this must have been terrifying. But even at eight, Jeanette demonstrated a will of steel.

If I had been amazed by her self-determination before, I was astounded by her presence of mind and raw courage in wrestling with this tiger-of-a-disease.

When she was confined to the iron lung, the doctors told my sister that she would probably spend the rest of her life there. But they reckoned without her spectacular courage. She announced firmly that she would NOT stay in the iron lung, and, moreover, that she would walk again! Shortly after this pronouncement, it was discovered that the virus had not affected her lungs, as previously thought, and that she could breathe on her own. Mercifully, she was released from her iron prison and consigned into a second hell.

She graduated to a wheelchair.

Because the virus had attacked the muscles in her legs and threatened to paralyze them, Jeanette was forced to spend entire days sitting in water as hot as she could stand it, with boards strapped to her legs to straighten them. This was torture enough, but nothing compared to the hot wet blanket treatment she endured for hours at a time.

Later, she described it to me.

"There were olive colored wool blankets that were put into some kind of metal steamer to make them as hot as possible." Nurses wrapped them around my legs and they felt horrible—hot, rough and tingly. I hated them."

About this time, the doctors informed my sister that she should get used to the idea of spending the rest of her life in a wheelchair, and that she would never walk again, to which the indomitable Jeanette replied: "I WILL, too, walk!"

The days of treatment turned into weeks and then months. Throughout her ordeal, Jeanette's indefatigable will never wavered. She amazed the doctors and nurses by telling everyone that she was going to walk again, repeating it over and over like a mantra or a prayer. As she progressed from iron lung to wheelchair to crutches, she was fierce in her determination to use her own legs.

"I WILL walk," she promised, and made such improvement that the customary braces many people with polio must wear were never even an option for her.

When she graduated to crutches, she was told that she would probably spend the rest of her life using these aids. Not surprisingly, she told the nurses and her family, "I will walk without crutches," and painstakingly proceeded to do so.

When she moved from crutches to a cane, she informed everyone that she would soon be walking without a cane. True to form, she systematically worked to retire the cane. Her family, friends and the now-convinced medical staff cheered her on. When her cane was discarded, she walked with a pronounced limp on her right side, turning her foot inward.

"I will walk without limping," she declared, and set about getting rid of the limp.

She became a familiar figure in the big hospital; a small girl taking determined steps along the hallways every day, all day, willing her foot to turn outward.

Three months or so after the initial diagnosis, my sister Jeanette came home from the hospital all by herself. She had convinced the doctors that she should be allowed to travel without a nurse, that she could walk alone, and, moreover, that she had earned the right to a homecoming of her design. She rode the twenty-three miles in a white ambulance with the siren sounding every step of the way, a small smile of satisfaction on her face.

When they arrived and the ambulance driver helped her out, she ascended the eleven concrete steps up the hill to my grandmother's porch, shaky, but unaided.

School was nearly out for the summer, so I did not witness the moment of her homecoming, but my grandmother did. She turned, saw Jeanette walk through th front door, and burst into tears of joy.

To this day, my brave sister will not wear knee-high boots. She says they remind her of the confining blankets and bandages she was forced to wear to straighten her legs. Although both legs were affected, her right leg was worse. It is slightly shorter than the other leg, but true to her word, she now walks in high heels without a limp, and if she didn't tell people, no one would ever know that she once had polio and nearly lost her ability to walk.

Jeanette finds it interesting that she shares a January 30th birthday with Franklin Delano Roosevelt, the only United States President who held four terms in office.

They have much in common. Both manifested an indomitable will. Both survived polio. Both went on to live vital, productive lives.

Jeanette will always be a heroine in my eyes because of the strength and fortitude she showed in the face of adversity. She taught me the meaning of courage and determination at an early age.

She demonstrated, stunningly, the powers of the mind. She showed that a person can bring about positive results from a seemingly negative situation through consistent, persistent use of the will: my sister, Rachel Jeanette Stevens, the bravest sister of all.

Judith Stevens is a poet and writer living in Virginia Beach, Virginia. She is executive director of the Citizen's Committee to Protect the Elderly, a non-profit grassroots advocacy group that is committed to raising the level of care in area nursing homes and assisted living facilities. Her latest article, "Nature as Healer," was published in the magazine Venture Inward, *and she is currently working on a new book on economic healing entitled,* The Dance of Abundance.

The Helen Keller Foundation for Research and Education continues the work to which its namesake dedicated her life. It's from her achievements that we draw our inspiration. And our global efforts to end blindness and deafness through medical research are a result of her belief that no matter what the obstacle anything is possible.

Our Mission Statement

Based on the legacy of Helen Keller, the Foundation strives to prevent blindness and deafness by advancing research and education. The Foundation aspires to be a leader in integrating sight, speech and hearing research with the greater biomedical research community, creating and coordinating a peer-reviewed, worldwide network of investigators and institutions.

Our Values and Beliefs

* We are inspired by and dedicated to the legacy of Helen Keller.
* We are aware of the optimism, courage, and perseverance needed to meet her calls to action.
* We are committed to integrating research and education with medical care and rehabilitation to prevent blindness and deafness, and to alleviate sight and hearing loss.
* We believe that research will substantially reduce the worldwide societal impact of sight and hearing loss.

Our Goals

* Integrate laboratory and clinical research to advance the state of vision and hearing research worldwide.
* Conduct a program of public education on the legacy of Helen Keller emphasizing vision and hearing awareness and the importance of medical research.
* Develop funding resources and a public relations effort sufficient to support an effective global research and education program.

Board of Directors and Officers

Charles Boswell (Chairman)
John Bradford (Treasurer)
Bill Edmonds
Roger Gehri
Warren Johnson
Ronald Levitt (Secretary)
Robert Morris (President)
Christopher Paterson, Ph.D., D.Sc.
C. Douglas Witherspoon, M.D.

The future of publishing...today!

Apprentice House is the country's only campus-based, student-staffed book publishing company. Directed by professors and industry professionals, it is a nonprofit activity of the Communication Department at Loyola College in Maryland.

Using state-of-the-art technology and an experiential learning model of education, Apprentice House publishes books in untraditional ways. This dual responsibility as publishers and educators creates an unprecedented collaborative environment among faculty and students, while teaching tomorrow's editors, designers, and marketers.

Outside of class, progress on book projects is carried forth by the AH Book Publishing Club, a co-curricular campus organization supported by Loyola College's Office of Student Activities.

Student Project Team for *Reading Lips*:
    Allyson Carroll, '08
    Gavie Heller, '08
    Mercedes Merrit, '07
    Marla Salezze, '07

Eclectic and provocative, Apprentice House titles intend to entertain as well as spark dialogue on a variety of topics.

Contributions are welcomed to sustain the press's work and are tax deductible to the fullest extent allowed by the IRS.

To learn more about Apprentice House books or to obtain submission guidelines, please visit www.ApprenticeHouse.com (made possible by the generous support and creativity of Mission Media).

Apprentice House
c/o Communication Department
Loyola College in Maryland
4501 N. Charles Street
Baltimore, MD 21210
Ph: 410-617-5265
Fax: 410-617-5040
info@apprenticehouse.com

Printed in the United States
121195LV00002B/10/P

9 781934 074190